SURVEY RESEARCH
FOR
PUBLIC
ADMINISTRATION

*To my wife, Brenda, whose love,
patience, and encouragement helped immeasurably*

SURVEY RESEARCH
FOR
PUBLIC
ADMINISTRATION

DAVID H. FOLZ

SAGE Publications
International Educational and Professional Publisher
Thousand Oaks   London   New Delhi

For information address:

SAGE Publications, Inc.
2455 Teller Road
Thousand Oaks, California 91320
E-mail: order@sagepub.com

SAGE Publications Ltd.
6 Bonhill Street
London EC2A 4PU
United Kingdom

SAGE Publications India Pvt. Ltd.
M-32 Market
Greater Kailash I
New Delhi 110 048 India

Printed in the United States of America

Library of Congress Cataloging-in-Publication Data

Folz, David H.
  Survey research for public administration / by David H. Folz.
    p. cm.
  Includes bibliographical references and index.
  ISBN 0-7619-0152-3 (acid-free paper). — ISBN 0-7619-0153-1
(pbk.: acid-free paper)
  1. Public opinion polls.   2. Public administration—Research.
I. Title.
HM261.F65   1996
303.3'8—dc20   95-50178

This book is printed on acid-free paper

95 96 97 98 99 10 9 8 7 6 5 4 3 2 1
Sage Production Editor: Diane S. Foster

Contents

List of Figures   ix

List of Tables   xi

Acknowledgments   xiii

1. Introduction   1
   Why Do a Citizen Survey?   1
   What Is a Citizen Survey?   2
   Purpose of This Book   2
   Decision Applications   3
       Policy Formulation   4
       Policy Implementation   4
       Policy Evaluation   4
       Surveys as Participation Mechanisms   7
   The Misuse of Citizen Surveys   7
   An Overview of the Survey Research Process   9
   Summary   12

2. Planning the Survey — 14

    Identifying the Survey's Objectives — 14

    What Can Surveys Tell Us? The Problem of Nonattitudes — 17

    Types of Information — 19

        Opinions and Attitudes — 19

        Beliefs and Perceptions — 21

        Behaviors — 21

        Facts and Attributes — 24

    Specifying Information Needs — 26

        Focus Groups — 28

        The Time Dimension — 29

    Identifying the Target Population — 30

    Methods of Contact: The Merits of Mail, Telephone,
       and Face-to-Face Surveys — 32

        Cost Considerations — 34

        Personnel Requirements — 36

        Implementation Time — 37

        Accuracy — 38

    Dealing With Nonresponses — 38

    Strategies for Surveying Elite or Specialized Populations — 39

    Summary — 41

3. Sampling — 42

    The Logic of Sampling — 43

    Determining Sample Size — 46

        Confidence Levels and Intervals — 47

        Small Populations — 49

        Analysis of Population Subgroups — 50

        Computing Sample Size — 50

    Sampling Designs — 52

    The Dangers of Nonprobability Sampling — 54

    Probability Sampling Methods — 57

        Simple Random Sampling — 57

        Systematic Sampling — 58

        Stratified Random Sampling — 59

        Cluster Sampling — 61

    Weighting Cases — 65

    Obtaining Samples for Telephone Surveys — 67

        Random Digit Dialing — 68

    Estimating the Size of the Sampling Pool for Telephone Surveys — 70

Screening Respondents for Telephone Interviews   71
Processing Sampling Pools   73
Calculating Response Rates   74
Summary   75

4. Survey Design and Implementation   77
   The Basics of Question Order   80
   Question Types   81
      Open-Ended Questions   81
      Closed-Ended Questions   83
   Choosing the Question Type   85
   Avoiding Bias in Questionnaire Design   87
   Composing Questions and Response Choices   91
      Positive Inducements   92
   Composition Standards   96
      Simplicity Versus Specificity   96
      Clarity   97
      Avoiding Biased Terms and Loaded Questions   101
      Time References   102
      Symmetry   102
   Question Order for Mail Surveys   103
   Constructing Indexes and Scales   105
   Designing the Mail Questionnaire   109
      The Cover Letter   109
      The Mail Questionnaire Booklet   110
   Implementing the Mailing   112
   Designing the Telephone Survey   115
      The Introductory Spiel   117
      Question Wording and Order for Telephone Surveys   118
   Pretesting the Questions and the Instrument   120
   Training Callers and Implementing the Telephone Survey   123
   Summary   125

5. Coding and Data Entry   127
   The Coding Process   128
      Selecting the Statistical Software   129
      The Coding Scheme   130
      Coding Open-Ended Questions   131
      The Codebook   132
   Data Entry   132

Computer-Assisted Telephone Interviewing	134
Data Cleaning	136
Summary	137
6. Data Analysis With Computers	138
A Statistical Primer	139
Levels of Measurement	140
Univariate Analysis	141
Presenting Survey Results in Tables	142
Measures of Central Tendency and Dispersion	144
Univariate Analysis With SPSS for Windows	145
Bivariate Analysis	147
Constructing Contingency Tables	148
Measures of Association and Statistical Significance	152
Multivariate Analysis: Controlling for Variables	162
Creating Charts to Summarize Findings	166
Summary	167
7. Preparing the Survey Report and Media Releases	172
The Survey Report	173
The Executive Summary	173
Survey Objectives	173
Methodology	173
Major Findings	174
Implications of the Findings	174
Media Releases	175
Summary	178
Appendix A: Random Numbers Table	179
Appendix B: Call Sheet	180
References	181
Index	183
About the Author	193

List of Figures

Figure 1.1. Survey Questions on Policy Formulation Issues   5
Figure 1.2. Survey Questions on Policy Implementation Issues   6
Figure 1.3. Questions on Service Evaluation Issues   8
Figure 1.4. Stages of the Survey Research Process   10

Figure 2.1. Questions That Elicit Opinions and Attitudes   20
Figure 2.2. Questions That Elicit Beliefs and Perceptions   22
Figure 2.3. Questions About Citizens' Behaviors   23
Figure 2.4. Examples of Attribute and Background Questions   26

Figure 3.1. Key Elements in Selecting a Probability Sample   44

Figure 4.1. An Overview of the Survey Design Process   79
Figure 4.2. Closed-Ended Questions With Ordered
             and Unordered Choices   86
Figure 4.3. Revising a Mail Questionnaire   94
Figure 4.4. Improving Question Clarity   97

Figure 4.5. Fixing Double-Barreled Questions   99
Figure 4.6. Balancing Response Choices   103
Figure 4.7. Items in an Index for Perceptions
    of a Downtown's Image   107
Figure 4.8. Mail Questionnaire Page Format   111
Figure 4.9. Example of a Cover Letter for a First Mailing   113
Figure 4.10. Example of a Cover Letter for a Second Mailing   114
Figure 4.11. Basic Format for an Introductory Spiel
    and Alternative Selection Criteria   118

Figure 5.1. Variable Definition Screen in SPSS for Windows   129
Figure 5.2. Excerpts From a Codebook for a Telephone
    Survey on Household Recycling Behaviors   133
Figure 5.3. A Data File Created in SPSS for Windows   134

Figure 6.1. Selecting Variables to Compute
    Frequency Distributions and Univariate
    Statistics With SPSS for Windows   146
Figure 6.2. SPSS for Windows Output From
    Frequencies Procedure   147
Figure 6.3. SPSS for Windows Crosstabs Procedure   150
Figure 6.4. SPSS for Windows Crosstabs Procedure Output   151
Figure 6.5. Selection of Statistics for a Crosstabulation
    in SPSS for Windows   157
Figure 6.6. Statistics Output for SPSS for Windows
    Crosstabulation Procedure   158
Figure 6.7. Examples of Chart Types   168

Figure 7.1. Hypothetical Press Release   177

List of Tables

Table 2.1. Key Decisions in the Survey Planning Process   15
Table 2.2. Relative Merits and Rankings of Mail, Telephone,
    and Face-to-Face Surveys on Selected Criteria   34

Table 3.1. Sample Sizes for Specified Levels of Precision,
    95% Confidence Interval   52
Table 3.2. Sample Sizes for Specified Levels of Precision,
    99.7% Confidence Interval   53
Table 3.3. Selecting Blocks With a Probability Proportionate
    to Size   64
Table 3.4. The Merits of Probability Sampling Strategies   66

Table 4.1. The Merits of Open-Ended and
    Closed-Ended Questions   88
Table 4.2. Guidelines for Constructing Mail Questionnaires   110
Table 4.3. Guidelines for Composing a Cover Letter   112

Table 6.1. Frequency and Percentage Distributions   143
Table 6.2. Levels of Measurement and Univariate Statistics   144
Table 6.3. Procedures and Statistics for Bivariate Analyses   149
Table 6.4. Sample Contingency Table: Popular Support
    in June 1999 for Citywide Curbside Recycling
    by Educational Attainment (in percentages)   152
Table 6.5. Multivariate Crosstabulation   164
Table 6.6. Illustration Objectives and Most
    Appropriate Chart Types   167

Acknowledgments

I owe a very special thanks to Gay Lyons, whose careful editorial scrutiny improved the readability of the text. My colleagues John Scheb and Lilliard Richardson in the Department of Political Science at the University of Tennessee, Knoxville, offered valuable advice and suggestions for the statistics and sampling chapters. Grant Neely, senior research assistant with the University of Tennessee Social Science Research Institute, provided critical research assistance. I also owe a debt of gratitude to my hardworking graduate assistants Rashmi Bora-Das and Erin Goewey, who helped with the innumerable tasks that accompany production of a book. I also want to thank the graduate students in my research methods seminars during 1994 and 1995, whose feedback on these chapters helped me greatly to refine explanations and examples. Finally, I am grateful to Peter Labella, political science editor at Sage Publications, who saw merit in this work, and to the anonymous reviewers who rendered many valuable suggestions.

1

Introduction

Why Do a Citizen Survey?

What do citizens think about the quality of the services they receive? Are clients having trouble getting the kind of help they want? Will residents in a neighborhood support the construction nearby of a new group home for the developmentally disabled? How often will people use a proposed recreation center? Will a plan to revitalize the central business district really bring more shoppers downtown? How many citizens can be relied on to take their recyclables to drop-off centers? Is there a need to change patrol strategies to improve the visibility of local law enforcement? What are people willing to pay for access to the information superhighway? Is it the right time to put a sales tax increase to a public vote? Do Medicaid patients think they have to wait too long to see a physician? Will citizens support service cutbacks to balance the budget?

Carefully crafted surveys can yield an abundance of useful information on these and a variety of other topics and issues of interest to decision makers in the public service. Having accurate information about what customers think can enable public administrators to make informed decisions and policy choices and to implement service improvements that respond to citizens' needs and preferences.

What Is a Citizen Survey?

There are several methods for discovering what people think. One of the best ways is to ask people directly about their opinions, but personal interviews are expensive and time-consuming, especially in large populations or among difficult-to-reach groups. A more practical method is to ask a sample, or a representative subset, of citizens about their opinions, attitudes, perceptions, and behaviors. A citizen survey uses a systematic, scientific method for selecting a sample of citizens, collecting information from them, and making generalizations about a larger population that is usually too large to observe or interview directly.

Opinion surveys are an accurate, affordable way to determine what large groups of people think. Many public administrators conduct such surveys regularly to identify budget priorities; to obtain feedback from citizens, customers, or clients on services and programs; and to acquire information on a variety of issues, problems, and choices that confront their organizations.

The prevalence of opinion surveys is one indicator of their popularity and potential for informing a variety of decisions that relate to management, accountability, and resource allocation. However, not all surveys are equally useful. Some meet the highest standards of scientific rigor, but others are a waste of time and money. The latter are those that include poorly written or misleading questions, omit important questions, or have flawed sampling designs. Only if a survey instrument is properly designed and implemented can it yield accurate information about who thinks what and why. Improperly designed and executed surveys can misrepresent respondents' views, and thus can mislead and confound decision making. That is why it is imperative that those who conduct citizen surveys understand and apply the guidelines that will produce scientifically valid and reliable survey data.

Purpose of This Book

This book describes a process for obtaining valid and reliable information from a citizen survey. It is intended to help public administrators become astute producers and consumers of public opinion surveys. It is written for readers who do not have substantial background in survey research or statistics. Some proficiency in operating a personal computer will enable the reader to complete the types of statistical analyses described.

The fundamental premise of the book is this: *Do it right, or don't bother to do it at all.* By *Do it right,* I mean plan, design, and implement surveys according to procedures that will produce survey questions that are *valid* (i.e., that will measure what one wants to measure), *reliable* (i.e., that will produce consistent results), and *useful* (i.e., that will yield the information needed).

The second premise of the book is that it is entirely possible to "do it right" within the resource constraints that confront most public administrators. The guidelines provided here will help researchers to design and implement high-quality opinion surveys without spending thousands of dollars for outside consultants. Of course, "in-house" surveys are not cost-free. The final cost of any project will depend primarily on how quickly the information is needed, the type of survey conducted, how difficult it is to reach the target population, how much confidence the researcher needs to have in the precision of the results, and the kind of software, hardware, and talent pool that exists in the organization. Managers of small organizations without any personnel available to conduct telephone interviews, for instance, may choose to design questionnaires in-house and then contract with polling firms to implement them. Administrators who do not have access to statistical software may seek out university public service consultants for technical assistance.

The essential point is that careful attention to the *details* of questionnaire design and implementation is required if a survey is to obtain valid, reliable, and useful information. Scores of public organizations successfully conduct surveys with just in-house personnel and perhaps some advice from consultants at universities or other public service organizations. Anyone can replicate such experiences by applying the principles of good survey research. One of the most fundamental of these is to invest the time needed to prepare a plan for the survey project that will help determine whether the project can be accomplished wholly or partly with existing resources. This book offers some practical advice for the managers who make these decisions.

Decision Applications

Survey information can help public officials to address issues in each of the stages of the policy process. It is helpful to begin the initial task of drafting questions by deciding whether the information desired is related mainly to policy formulation, implementation, or evaluation. Inevitably, there is some overlap among these stages, as the questions in this chapter illustrate, but they provide a useful initial framework for thinking about information needs and the kinds of decisions that can be informed by survey results. It is also useful to consider how opinion surveys can help to broaden the scope of citizen participation in the variety of decisions that confront officials in the public arena.

POLICY FORMULATION

Policy formulation involves deciding what to do. Surveys can help public officials to determine what people need, want, prefer, or demand from their government or for their tax dollars. They can then use this information as they make choices, set priorities, change practices, and translate popular demands into public policy. Questions that help to inform policy choices often measure the preferences, popularity, or acceptability of singular or competing ideas, actions, choices, or services. Figure 1.1 gives examples of the kinds of questions with import for policy formulation that might be included in a mail or telephone survey.

POLICY IMPLEMENTATION

Surveys also can help public officials decide how best to deliver or provide services. Useful questions in this area may concern the variety of activities and decisions involved in implementing a policy, program, or service. These can be directed to one or more of the groups with a stake in the issue, such as elected officials, citizen's advisory boards, the public employees responsible for a service, the management team, or service recipients.

As long as the respondents have some knowledge or information about an implementation issue, the questions asked may concern just about any type of goal, project, proposal, or service. The questions in Figure 1.2, for instance, might be prepared by managers who want to devise a plan to improve a city building permit process.

POLICY EVALUATION

Citizen surveys can also provide useful feedback for evaluation of public policies and programs. In the business of service delivery, the consumer's

For a mail survey:

1. If the city were forced to reduce expenditures to achieve a balanced budget, which of the following services or programs do you think should be reduced in funding **first**? (Circle the number of your choice.)

    1 FIRE PROTECTION
    2 POLICE PROTECTION
    3 PARKS AND RECREATION
    4 STREET MAINTENANCE
    5 DON'T KNOW/ NOT SURE

2. Which of the following actions do you think will contribute the **most** to the beautification of Union City? (Circle one.)

    1 ADOPT STRICTER ARCHITECTURAL CONTROLS
    2 PLANT TREES AND SHRUBS ALONG MAIN STREET
    3 CLEAR BRUSH ALONG STREETS
    4 IMPLEMENT NEIGHBORHOOD ANTILITTER CAMPAIGNS
    5 CONSTRUCT BICYCLE AND WALKING TRAILS

3. To what extent, if at all, is each of the following a problem in your neighborhood? (Circle the number that corresponds to your rating of each item.)

Condition	No Problem	Minor Problem	Major Problem
Unmowed vacant lots	1	2	3
Houses in disrepair	1	2	3
Sidewalks in disrepair	1	2	3
Noisy animals	1	2	3
Street litter	1	2	3
Abandoned vehicles	1	2	3
Traffic congestion	1	2	3

For a telephone interview:

1. Do you oppose or favor the consolidation of the City of Knoxville and Knox County governments into one metropolitan government? Would you say that you: [READ CHOICES]

    1 STRONGLY OPPOSE
    2 OPPOSE
    3 NEITHER OPPOSE NOR FAVOR
    4 FAVOR
    5 STRONGLY FAVOR

Figure 1.1. Survey Questions on Policy Formulation Issues

perception is the pertinent reality. Even the most efficient department is not doing its job well if citizens are not satisfied with the various dimensions of output effectiveness, such as the quality, timeliness, level, accuracy, reliability, convenience, utility, and price of the service. Citizens' perceptions

For a self-administered survey of city employees in the permit center:
1. During January through March of this year, did you hear any complaints expressed by applicants for a city building permit?

    1 No
    2 Yes

    1a. If "Yes," please circle the number(s) next to the complaints you heard:

        1 The high cost of the building permit
        2 The long wait in line to receive information about city regulations
        3 The confusing nature of the building regulations
        4 The time required to decide whether to issue a permit or not
        5 The strict nature of the regulations
        6 Other (please explain):_____

2. In the performance of your job responsibilities, how helpful do *you* think it would be to have computer access to the planning department's land use database?

    1 Not at all helpful
    2 Somewhat helpful
    3 Very helpful
    4 Not sure/don't know

3. Would you be willing to participate in a cross-training program for Permit Center personnel that would enable you to answer citizen inquiries about any of the city's building and zoning codes?

    1 No
    2 Yes
    3 Don't know/not sure

For a telephone interview of members of the city builders' association:
1. Did you apply for a city building permit at any time during 1995? [READ CHOICES]

    1 No
    2 Yes [IF YES, ASK QUESTIONS 1a and 1b]

    1a. About how long did it take the city to process your last permit application?

        1 Less than 1 business day
        2 1 to 2 business days
        3 3 to 4 business days
        4 5 to 6 business days
        5 More than 6 business days

    1b. Were you satisfied or not with the time it required the city to process your permit application? Would you say that you were: [READ CHOICES]
        1 Dissatisfied
        2 Neither satisfied nor dissatisfied
        3 Satisfied

Figure 1.2. Survey Questions on Policy Implementation Issues

about the effectiveness of public services should count for much in the calculus of a department's service productivity. Delivering services that are both responsive *and* efficient is, of course, the dual challenge that confronts managers.

Survey questions can ascertain *what* citizens think about the quality of services, *who* uses services, *how* frequently they use them, and *where* specific improvements need to be made. Public administrators can then make resource adjustments before problems become crises. For example, survey findings might suggest the need to publicize the availability of services that are underutilized. The feedback obtained from consumers or prospective clients can identify areas of strength, weakness, and needed improvement. Figure 1.3 offers examples of service evaluation questions.

SURVEYS AS PARTICIPATION MECHANISMS

Surveys can help to broaden the scope of citizens' participation in government decision making. Practitioners know that citizens who feel they play a part in or have some impact upon a policy or program are more likely to feel they have a stake in its outcome. Opinion surveys enable local officials to determine *who* thinks *what* and *why* with respect to a program or project. A survey is one means by which the "voices" of those who do not typically show up at community meetings can be heard. If citizens feel that public officials care about and consider their views before taking action or implementing a program, they are more likely to feel they have some stake in the success of the policy or program.

Citizen surveys are one means of advancing a process of deliberative democracy, where public officials address citizens' concerns up front rather than later, in court. As a method of practicing the politics of inclusion, surveys have the potential to enhance the quality of democratic governance. This potential can be realized when the objectives of the survey are clear, when citizens have enough information to make choices and to form opinions, and when the findings are publicized and discussed in forums of community outreach.

The Misuse of Citizen Surveys

Surveys are misused in a variety of ways and are sometimes employed to defraud or dupe people. Surveys should never substitute for popular referenda on issues. Polls should never substitute for popular votes, because they cannot satisfy the relevant legal standard of one person, one vote.

Surveys should never be performed just to obtain "ammunition" for or against particular causes or actions. The instruments used in such surveys almost always contain loaded or biased questions. Citizens are quite able

1. During 1995, did you call the Oak Ridge city police department to request an officer's assistance?

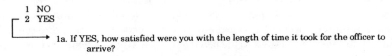

    1   NO
    2   YES

    1a. If YES, how satisfied were you with the length of time it took for the officer to arrive?

        1   VERY DISSATISFIED
        2   DISSATISFIED
        3   NEITHER SATISFIED NOR DISSATISFIED
        4   SATISFIED
        5   VERY SATISFIED

2. For 1996, how would you rate the quality of each of the following services that the city of Arlington provided in your neighborhood? (Please circle the number of your choice.)

Service	VERY POOR	POOR	NEITHER GOOD NOR POOR	GOOD	EXCELLENT
POTHOLE PATCHING	1	2	3	4	5
GARBAGE COLLECTION	1	2	3	4	5
PARK MAINTENANCE	1	2	3	4	5
LEAF COLLECTION	1	2	3	4	5
POLICE PATROL	1	2	3	4	5

Alternatively, respondents can be asked to check the box next to their response:
3. Did you use the metropolitan bus system anytime during 1996?

    1 ☐   No
    2 ☐   Yes   (If "Yes," please answer 3a and 3b.)

    3a. If "Yes," about how often did your bus arrive at its scheduled time? (Please check one.)

        1 ☐   Never
        2 ☐   Rarely
        3 ☐   Sometimes
        4 ☐   Most of the time
        5 ☐   Always

  → 3b. How satisfied were you with the general cleanliness of the bus(es) in which you rode?

        1 ☐   Satisfied
        2 ☐   Dissatisfied
        3 ☐   Don't know/ Not sure

Figure 1.3. Questions on Service Evaluation Issues

to detect questions that just do not sound right or that are slanted to obtain desired responses. An example would be a survey question that asks respondents simply whether they support a universal health care program, without ascribing any cost implications or likely impacts on existing health insurance coverage. Questions designed solely to achieve some partisan political aim should be avoided.

Obviously, survey findings on controversial topics will be used by different groups to reinforce their views, but those who design and write survey questions must never bring preconceived notions, biases, or hidden agendas to the task. Survey designers should make every effort to develop questions that will elicit what people really think, not what the survey sponsor hopes they think.

Surveys should not be used to collect information that is already available from published sources. A policy maker may need information about home values or utility hookups, for example, but such data are available from the existing records of the property assessor's office and relevant utility companies. It is usually much less expensive to unearth existing data than it is to conduct surveys to obtain them.

Increasingly common misuses of surveys are "sugging," or selling by telemarketers under the guise of survey research, and "frugging," or fundraising under the guise of research (Rubenstein, 1995). Another regrettable misuse involves political canvassing to identify the names, addresses, and phone numbers of citizens for later sale to political or marketing concerns without the informed consent of the respondents. These practices are unethical. Survey researchers should adhere to the professional code of ethics and practices published by the American Association for Public Opinion Research (1986). These guidelines suggest standards for scientific competence and integrity in conducting, analyzing, and reporting survey research and recommend procedures to protect the confidentiality of responses and the anonymity of survey respondents.

An Overview of the Survey Research Process

The survey research process involves eight major stages: planning, sampling, survey design, staff organization and training, pretesting, data coding and processing, data analysis, and writing of reports and media releases. The content and methods of each of these stages make up the basic organizational framework of the book. The general sequence of these stages is illustrated in Figure 1.4, but several tasks within each stage can be performed simultaneously, depending upon staff resources and experience.

Planning. The ultimate success of a survey hinges on several key decisions made during the planning stage. These include defining the purpose(s) of

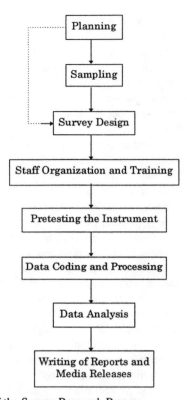

Figure 1.4. Stages of the Survey Research Process

the survey, determining what type of information is needed and how the information will be used, specifying who will be surveyed, deciding what type of survey (mail, telephone, or personal interview) will best fulfill the survey objectives, and determining the personnel and other resources needed to design, manage, and implement the survey.

Sampling. The heart of a scientific sampling process is *random selection.* This involves selecting a subset of *cases,* such as people, addresses, or phone numbers, from the population about which one wants to generalize so that every case in that population has an equal or known chance of being included in the survey. Random selection techniques enable the researcher to establish a level of confidence and error margin within which the results obtained are likely to represent the entire population.

Sampling is one of the most rigorous aspects of scientific survey research. To minimize bias, the researcher must preserve the random nature of the selection of individuals or cases for inclusion in a survey. An *unbiased sample* is one in which no group or class of individuals is systematically under- or overrepresented. The quality of any survey in which a sample is selected is generally distinguished by how that sample is obtained.

Survey design. The design stage is perhaps the most challenging aspect of survey research. In this stage, the researcher must make decisions about what types of questions to ask and how best to phrase them. How well he or she accomplishes these tasks will determine whether the objectives of the survey are fulfilled. Ultimately, the issues of validity, reliability, accuracy, and response rate depend upon the choices made about question type, format, wording, order, number, coding, instructions, sequence, and appearance. Preparation of a cover letter for a mail survey or an introductory spiel for a telephone interview is another task integral to survey design.

Staff organization and training. At the outset of a survey project, the researcher must determine who should do what, when, and how. Clear task assignments, staff training, and performance monitoring are key responsibilities of the project manager. Quality control strategies are described in Chapter 4.

Pretesting of the instrument. Changing questions once a survey is under way will jeopardize the validity and reliability of the entire project. Survey designers should ask their planned questions of a small number of those in the population of interest *before* questionnaires are printed up or any telephone interviews are initiated, in order to detect possible problems in question clarity, meaning, order, or instructions. Nothing is more frustrating for a researcher than realizing that respondents have consistently misinterpreted the meaning of a question. Questions should be worded so that there is no ambiguity about their meaning, because this directly affects the validity of the responses. A question about the "volume" of solid waste produced, for instance, should not lead respondents to think that the question refers to how much noise garbage trucks make. Likewise, asking for "the number of people in your household broken down by sex" will bring only derision from respondents with a sardonic sense of humor. The general admonition about survey design is this: *Pretest the questionnaire!*

Data coding and processing. In this context, *coding* refers to the way questions and responses are reduced to numerical terms. *Processing* refers to the procedures used to create a data set so that survey responses can be transformed into usable information. Creating a data file enables the researcher to take advantage of the power of statistical software programs to perform analyses on a large number of responses swiftly and accurately.

Data analysis. The kinds of statistical analyses needed will depend on the purposes and objectives of the survey. Every report should include frequency distributions and properly constructed tables that portray the important findings. These tables may report simple percentage distributions or display the nature of a relationship between two variables, controlling for the effects of a third factor. Univariate statistics describe and summarize the responses to survey questions. Exploring who thinks what, and why, requires the use of bivariate and multivariate statistics appropriate for the number of variables and the level of their measurement. To understand the relationships among variables, and to help decision makers interpret the survey findings, it is important for the researcher to know when it is appropriate to use certain statistics and how to interpret them.

Writing of reports and media releases. Surveys are useless unless their results and implications are communicated clearly and succinctly. Researchers need to develop the considerable skill required to prepare useful final reports, informative executive summaries, and clear, concise media releases. Such media releases, in particular, can minimize misinterpretations and provide the basis on which nontechnical audiences can judge the survey's quality and utility.

Summary

A well-planned, carefully designed, and efficiently implemented survey can provide public officials with information they need to make better, or at least more informed, decisions in the public policy process. Whether the chief concern is to improve management, enhance accountability, or make better resource allocation decisions, good surveys are one means by which we can advance our understanding of popular opinions, preferences, and beliefs.

Devising a good survey instrument is both an art and a science, and a primary tool of the trade is language. Composing questions and designing a questionnaire are two steps in the process that will challenge a researcher's creative resources. If the product survives the crucibles of clarity, scientific accuracy, and validity, the survey's information objectives will be attained.

2

Planning the Survey

Identifying the Survey's Objectives

Surveys can be expensive, but careful planning can help to minimize costs. Before the first question is written, it is imperative that the designer determine the purpose and objectives of the survey, how the information will be obtained and used, and who will be responsible for managing the survey project. This chapter describes the key decisions that should be made during the survey planning process.

This process is not as tidy as the list presented in Table 2.1 suggests, because considerable time, many meetings, and several drafts usually are necessary to achieve consensus on decisions critical to the success of the survey enterprise. The table gives an overview of the key decisions and considerations in planning a survey and lists some of the methods that public administrators can use to facilitate these decisions.

The first challenge for the survey designer is to get the sponsors to specify what they want to know and why they want to know it. It is likely that several meetings will need to be held for discussion of drafts of survey

TABLE 2.1 Key Decisions in the Survey Planning Process

Reach a consensus on the purposes and objectives of the survey.
  Considerations
    What are the links to issues in the stages of the policy process?
    Is the purpose chiefly to explore, describe, or explain various phenomena?
  Methods
    Workshops
    Brainstorming sessions
    Nominal group techniques
Specify information needs.
  Considerations
    Review the types of information that survey questions can measure, and use these to
      classify information objectives.
    What problems might arise with "nonattitudes" among the target population?
    Time: Is the survey a one-time cross-sectional effort or part of an ongoing longitudinal study?
    Specify the major dependent and independent variables for later analysis.
  Methods
    Focus groups
    Literature review
    Workshops to review drafts of information objectives and "ideal" items of information
      desired
Identify the target population.
  Considerations
    Determine the unit of analysis.
    What kinds of screen or filter questions are needed to obtain information from knowledge-
      able respondents?
    What population attributes are important for the study?
    How difficult will it be to contact the desired target population?
  Methods
    List the types of information needed from various population groups and the kinds of
      analyses required to determine who thinks what and why. Check to ensure that the
      intended unit of analysis corresponds with the level of information needed.
    Research availability of accurate lists or investigate the cost of purchasing lists from a
      sampling firm.
Select the method(s) of contact.
  Considerations
    Review the merits of mail, telephone, and face-to-face surveys.
    Determine when survey results are needed.
    Establish desired confidence level and interval if a sample is to be selected.
    Balance available resources with estimated costs of the desired method of contact.
  Methods
    Ascertain the monetary amount available for the survey project, inventory personnel and
      staff skills, obtain estimates for cost of implementation by a private consultant (for
      comparison), and decide whether to adjust the time frame for the study, the desired con-
      fidence interval, and whether to contract out some part of the project's implementation.

objectives and information needs before clear agreement is reached on what the survey is supposed to accomplish. Without this consensus, it is difficult for the survey designer to know precisely what to ask, how to frame questions, and how to interpret the results. Failure to achieve consensus as to survey objectives will severely limit the utility of the survey results as a decision-making aid, and conducting such a survey is usually a waste of resources. Once the survey designer has identified specific information needs and objectives, he or she can begin selecting the best types of question structure and wording.

What are some typical survey purposes? As described in Chapter 1, they may embrace issues related to one or more of the phases of the policy process. The specific purpose of a given survey, for example, may be to identify perceptions about community needs or priorities, or to gather data that will help officials gauge popular support for a specific action, design better services, or assess how well a program works. Another way to think about the purpose of a survey is to consider whether its primary function is to explore, describe, or explain some phenomenon or topic. *Exploratory* survey questions measure some behavior, opinion, or event that is not well understood and about which decision makers would like to know more. What do different groups in the community think about a proposed school choice policy? Will citizens be willing to accept a volume-based pricing system for solid waste disposal? Other questions may seek to *describe* some population or group. Who uses the library? How many citizens live in the annexed territory? What is the nature of employee experiences with the new HMO?

Understanding the "why" behind various behaviors, attitudes, or events is the purpose of *explanatory* questions. Why do certain neighborhoods have more crime? Why are citizens opposed to metropolitan government? Why do more Americans believe they get more for their tax dollars from local and state governments than from the federal government?

The outcome of the survey researchers' meetings with the sponsors and those who intend to use the information produced by the survey should be a consensus on the basic objectives of the survey. These vary by organization, but some typical objectives include the following:

- Establish a hierarchy of community needs, problems, goals, and concerns.
- Determine what policies, programs, plans, or budget options citizens prefer, who supports what, and why.
- Evaluate the performance of, or demand for, various services, facilities, functions, events, and activities.

- Understand and explore various experiences, behaviors, attitudes, opinions, and characteristics of individuals or groups and how these change over time.
- Compare the attitudes, opinions, beliefs, and behaviors of different groups.

Survey results can be used by those who must plan and improve programs, prepare and justify budgets, gauge agency responsiveness, motivate program staff, or monitor and evaluate the performance of employees or contractors. Reaching agreement with sponsors beforehand on why certain information is needed helps the survey designer to clarify exactly what needs to be asked in the questionnaire.

To launch the planning process, it is helpful for the designer to prepare an ideal list of everything the survey sponsors would like to know about the target population. In all probability, this list will have to be pared down, guided by judgments about the relative importance of the survey objectives. It is always tempting to use a survey to ask a large number of questions about a wide variety of issues. Although such broad topical coverage is possible, there is a point of diminishing returns. Surveys that are too long, or that are perceived by respondents to be too long, risk substantial drop-off in participation. The process of deciding what to leave in and what to leave out may cause friction among different organizational interests, but no one wins if the length of the instrument discourages people from completing it.

The general rule is to keep mail surveys to a maximum of 12 page faces and telephone interviews to about 20 minutes or less. The best way to design a survey within these parameters is for the designer to justify inclusion of each question by determining how much it contributes to the central purpose and objectives of the survey (Dillman, 1978). Survey designers can hold workshops and brainstorming sessions among staff and sponsors to help prioritize survey objectives; they may need to employ nominal group techniques to attain consensus among particularly contentious interests.

What Can Surveys Tell Us?
The Problem of Nonattitudes

Before making decisions about question type and wording, the survey designer should ascertain whether a questionnaire is capable of gathering the data necessary to measure what sponsors wish to measure. The survey sponsors should recognize that not every issue of central importance to them will necessarily be a hot topic of discussion among folks at the local feed store, church, or supermarket. Knowledge of what surveys *can* measure should be tempered by the recognition that some citizens will be totally unfamiliar with certain topics. In fact, the chances are very good that many people have neither thought much about nor formed specific opinions on the various topics raised in the typical community survey.

The problem of *nonattitudes,* or getting responses that are merely superficial reactions to the interview or to the instrument itself, has been well documented (Asher, 1988; Norpoth & Lodge, 1985; Schuman & Presser, 1981) and should be a serious concern for questionnaire designers. People may answer questions even when they have no real views on the matters involved; they may simply wish not to be perceived as ignorant. Richard Morin (1995), reporting in the *Washington Post,* described a 1995 redux of an experiment conducted in 1978 by pollsters who asked, "Some people say the 1975 Public Affairs Act should be repealed. Do you agree or disagree that it should be repealed?" Of the 501 Americans surveyed, 24% agreed the act should be repealed, 19% disagreed, and a brave 57% expressed no opinion. The Public Affairs Act is fictitious; nonetheless, 43% of the respondents in this national poll expressed some opinion about it. Another stage of the experiment offered two different, randomly selected groups partisan cues in the question. The original wording "some people say" was replaced with either "President Clinton says" or "Republicans in Congress say." As Morin reports:

> You guessed it: more than half of those questioned offered an opinion when given a partisan cue. And Democrats were more likely to support repeal of the phantom act (and Republicans oppose) when told Clinton favored repeal—but Republicans were far more likely to favor repeal when cued that congressional GOPers favored dumping it.

Clearly, researchers have to be wary of measuring "pseudo-opinions" or popular reactions to factors other than what the researchers intend to measure. As Asher (1988) explains, even when a diligent effort is made to word questions properly, any information obtained from people who really do not or cannot be expected to have genuine opinions or attitudes should be suspect.

There are several techniques for dealing with the problem of nonattitudes. I review a few briefly here and offer more examples in Chapter 4. One of the best methods is to ask a *screen* or *filter* question that inquires whether the individual has heard or read anything about a particular topic that is the subject of the subsequent question. If the response is negative, the interviewer simply skips subsequent question(s) on that topic. Screen questions (see examples in Figures 2.1 and 2.3) ascertain whether people have knowledge about or experience with particular matters and are appropriate for mail, telephone, or personal interview formats. It is infinitely preferable to have a large proportion of "don't know" or "no opinion" responses than to treat nonattitude responses as if they measure genuine public opinions or behaviors.

Another technique for dealing with nonattitudes is to explain a particular proposal or idea in nonbiased terms before asking a question about it. For example: "The city is proposing to construct a $1.8 million multipurpose community center that would be paid for with existing sales tax revenue. The center would have an indoor pool, gym, and running track, among other things. Would you say that you strongly favor, favor, oppose, strongly oppose, or have no opinion about this proposed community center?"

A filtering process makes it more socially acceptable for respondents to indicate that they are unfamiliar with the topic of the question. Unless the objective is to measure *specifically* the extent of public knowledge about or awareness of a program or service, the target population should be familiar with the subjects covered by a questionnaire.

Types of Information

It is useful for the survey designer to think of questions as aimed at gathering information in one of four major categories: opinions or attitudes, beliefs or perceptions, behavior, and facts or attributes. Specifying the type of information sought by a question helps the researcher to create questions with the appropriate response categories.

OPINIONS AND ATTITUDES

Thoughts, feelings, and judgments about issues, events, problems, and policies are measured by questions that are evaluative in nature. What people like or dislike and how strongly they feel about issues are indicated by response choices that measure respondents' positive or negative orientations toward policy choices, issues, actions, problems, persons, and events.

Typically, public officials are interested in knowing about citizens' preferences for services, judgments about services, or evaluations of service quality or performance. The opinion distributions revealed by surveys enable public administrators to calculate the frequencies and

1. Do you think that the Oakland Police Department is doing enough to prevent crime in the city's public housing projects?

    1 NO
    2 YES
    3 DON'T KNOW/ NOT SURE

2. The police commissioner has proposed a bicycle patrol program for each of the city's public housing projects. What do you think of this idea? Would you say that you strongly oppose, oppose, favor, or strongly favor a police bicycle patrol program in the city's public housing projects?

    1 STRONGLY OPPOSE
    2 OPPOSE
    3 NEITHER OPPOSE NOR FAVOR
    4 FAVOR
    5 STRONGLY FAVOR
    6 DON'T KNOW/ NOT SURE

A screen question:
3. Would you be willing to pay an additional **3 cents** on the property tax *rate* for a bicycle patrol program in the city's public housing projects? This increase would add about $30 a year to the property tax bill for a $100,000 house.

    1 NO
    2 YES
    3 DON'T KNOW/ NOT SURE

    → [If NO, ask:] 3a. Would you be willing to pay an additional **2 cents** on the property tax *rate* for a bicycle patrol program in the city's public housing projects? This increase would add about $20 a year to the property tax bill for a $100,000 house.

    1 NO
    2 YES
    3 DON'T KNOW/ NOT SURE

4. Do you agree or disagree with this statement: "Parents of school-age children should be given vouchers by the state that can be used to pay for the cost of educating their children at **any** school in the county, public **or** private, of the parents' choice."

    1 STRONGLY DISAGREE
    2 DISAGREE
    3 NEITHER AGREE NOR DISAGREE
    4 AGREE
    5 STRONGLY AGREE

Figure 2.1. Questions That Elicit Opinions and Attitudes

proportions of respondents who favor or oppose particular actions, agree or disagree with given policies, or are satisfied or dissatisfied with particular services. Attitudes often are measured using indexes that consist of several questions about the various dimensions of some issue or phenomenon (index construction is explained in Chapter 4). Figure 2.1 provides examples of some questions that measure opinions and attitudes.

BELIEFS AND PERCEPTIONS

Questions concerned with respondents' beliefs and perceptions are designed to assess what they think is true or untrue, or what they believe exists or does not exist. No qualitative rating is implied in such questions. Belief questions measure what people perceive to be real and can be framed in the past, present, or future tense. For example, the following question is designed to elicit respondents' beliefs about future action to be taken by the city council: "Do you think the city council will raise the property tax to pay for increased costs of school bus transportation this school year?" Whether the council actually intends to raise the tax mentioned is unimportant; the question's purpose is to discover whether the respondent believes the council will act in a particular way.

Identifying popular perceptions about future events can help those who need to know who may support or oppose proposed actions. Asking residents, for example, whether they believe that a proposed new auto assembly plant in their area will actually produce the 1,000 new jobs promised by the manufacturer can provide useful information for both local officials and the auto company's executives, who may want to know whether they have a credibility problem.

Survey questions that measure beliefs can help local officials to understand what people think is true. Questions may be phrased to test people's knowledge about specific facts. For instance, asking citizens how often they think leaves and brush are picked up in their neighborhoods may reveal perceptions that indicate a need to publicize the collection schedule more widely.

Public administrators often need to determine which groups attach importance to various services and programs. Asking citizens what they perceive to be the most important problems, spending priorities, or needed service improvements can generate useful feedback for those who must make policy, budget, and personnel decisions. Figure 2.2 shows some questions designed to elicit information about beliefs and perceptions.

BEHAVIORS

Questions about behaviors inquire about what people have done in the past, what they are currently doing, or what they plan to do in the future. Explaining variations in behaviors (who does what, when, where, and why) is usually the central purpose for asking these types of questions. Behavior questions may cover many different topics, such as whether citizens take

1. Which of the following randomly listed items do you believe is the single **most** serious problem confronting the city of Bartlett this year?   (Please circle your choice.)

    1   CRIME
    2   UNEMPLOYMENT
    3   TRAFFIC CONGESTION
    4   INADEQUATE SCHOOL FACILITIES
    5   LOCAL TAX BURDEN

2. How important to you are each of the following factors in improving the quality of life in the city of Paris?   (Please circle the number of your rating for each factor.)

Factor	Not Important	Somewhat Important	Very Important
Stricter Land Use Controls	1	2	3
Preserving Historic Buildings	1	2	3
Developing More Parks	1	2	3
Revitalizing the Downtown Area	1	2	3
Attracting More Employment Opportunities	1	2	3
Holding the Line on Local Property Taxes	1	2	3
Increasing Housing Choice	1	2	3
Reducing Crime	1	2	3

3. For each of the following services or programs provided by the city of Germantown, do you think the city spends too little, about the right amount, or too much?   (Please circle the number of your choice.)

Service	Too Little	About Right	Too Much
Public Safety	1	2	3
Economic Development	1	2	3
Public Education	1	2	3
Street Maintenance	1	2	3
Sanitation Services	1	2	3

Figure 2.2. Questions That Elicit Beliefs and Perceptions

their recyclable materials to a drop-off center, how frequently they visit any of the city's recreational facilities, or whether they have been victims of crime during the preceding year. Figure 2.3 gives examples of behavioral questions.

A screen question for a telephone interview:
1. Did you play golf at the Sawgrass Course during 1996?

    1 NO
    2 YES [IF YES, ASK 1A AND 1B]
    3 NOT SURE/DON'T REMEMBER

        → 1a. About how many times did you play golf there during 1996?

        1 ONCE OR TWICE
        2 THREE OR FOUR TIMES
        3 FIVE OR SIX TIMES
        4 MORE THAN SIX TIMES

      1b. How would you rate the overall quality of grounds maintenance?

        1 POOR
        2 FAIR
        3 GOOD
        4 NOT SURE/NO OPINION

Another screen question for a telephone interview:
1. Did your household participate in Johnson City's curbside recycling program during May 1997?

    1 NO
    2 YES [IF YES, ASK 1A]
    3 NOT SURE/DON'T KNOW

        → 1a. Which of the following materials did your household place in the bins?

	NO	YES	NOT SURE
ALUMINUM CANS	1	2	3
CLEAR GLASS	1	2	3
NEWSPAPER	1	2	3
PLASTIC MILK JUGS	1	2	3
STEEL CANS	1	2	3

3. In talking to people in the city of Kingsport about the last city election, we found that some people did not vote because they weren't registered, were ill, or just didn't have the time. How about you? Did you vote in the last city election held in August 1996?

    1 NO
    2 YES
    3 NOT SURE

Figure 2.3. Questions About Citizens' Behaviors

When asked about their behaviors, people may give responses that are colored by a number of factors, including how well they recollect their past actions or nonactions, the perceived social desirability of certain kinds of behaviors (such as not wanting to admit that they do not vote), the sensitivity of the question's topic (such as not wanting to discuss an incident involving assault or rape), and the temporal context in which the question is asked (how long it has been since a particular incident occurred). Chapter 4 includes a discussion of how these factors affect the rate, quality, and interpretation of survey responses.

Questions concerning behaviors should be constructed so that they are relatively undemanding and nonthreatening. The question, "How many times did you play golf at the Sawgrass course in Pointe Vedra, Florida, during 1996?" can be made less demanding for the respondent if, rather than being expected to provide a specific number, he or she is provided with answer choices that include different frequency ranges. Likewise, answer choices made up of ranges are useful for making sensitive questions on income and age less threatening to respondents. As I explain in Chapter 4, it is preferable for researchers to use closed-ended questions when seeking this kind of information, as long as the response categories are *mutually exclusive* and *exhaustive* with respect to expected possible responses. People's natural reluctance to discuss sensitive topics can also be attenuated if they believe that their responses will be kept confidential. For this reason, it is important that the survey instrument's cover letter or spoken introduction establish the credibility of the person(s) or agency conducting the survey and assure the respondent of the confidentiality of his or her answers.

Survey designers must also be aware that unusual or unanticipated temporal circumstances or events can affect responses to some questions. The time frame of a question is especially sensitive in this regard. Suppose the researcher wants to know whether respondents participate in car or van pools. If the major employer in the area where the survey is administered dismisses a substantial proportion of the local workforce just prior to or during the time in which the survey is conducted, any work-related question on this topic that uses the word *currently* will produce a picture of commuter behavior decidedly different from a question that incorporates a common time frame, such as June 1996.

FACTS AND ATTRIBUTES

In virtually every survey, it is imperative to know *who* thinks or believes what, or who behaves in certain ways. For this reason, it is wise for survey designers to include questions about the respondent characteristics germane to the purpose of the survey. Information about who answers given questions in particular ways enhances the utility of the results for decision making. Although it is useful to know, for instance, that 70% of respondents favor a particular location for a new school, it may be even more important to know who does not support or favor that location. Are they residents who live in the immediate vicinity of the proposed site? Are they empty-nesters who do not have school-age children? Information about who thinks what can help officials to address the specific concerns of different groups.

Answers to attribute questions often form *independent variables* that help to explain variations in responses to questions that form *dependent variables,* which typically are questions about people's opinions, attitudes, beliefs, and behaviors. The relationships that emerge between independent and dependent variables enable those who use survey data to understand more completely not only who thinks, believes, and behaves in certain ways but also why they do so. Conversely, the answers to various attitude and opinion questions may form highly valuable independent variables in some studies that help to explain why residents choose to live where they do, or why they support or oppose various actions or policies.

The *selective* inclusion of attribute questions in a survey is vital if the researcher is to capitalize on the survey's total information potential. Because every survey project is different, there is no standard set of attribute questions that should be asked in all surveys. To save space and time, the designer should include only those attribute questions that are germane to the purposes of the particular survey.

Attribute questions generally gather the information used to measure a respondent's socioeconomic status (SES). Information on income, educational attainment, occupation, and homeownership can be useful for comparing respondents and their opinions. Attribute questions may also ascertain the respondent's race or ethnicity, place of residence, voting district, zip code, neighborhood, age, gender, household size, number of children under 18, and/or length of residence in a jurisdiction. Examples of typical attribute questions are shown in Figure 2.4.

Another very important reason researchers ask about the characteristics and backgrounds of respondents is so that they can determine whether or not a sample is *representative* of the entire population of interest. By comparing the profile of the respondents with that of the larger population, it is possible to ascertain how closely the two match. If there are no significant differences between a sample's attributes and those of the larger population from which the sample is drawn, then that sample is said to be representative. For this reason, it is important for the survey designer to include response categories for attribute questions that match the categories used by the U.S. Census. The questions on age, education, and income in Figure 2.4, for example, employ census response categories.

Transition statement:
Finally, we need to ask you a few questions so that your responses can be compared to those of other citizens in Maryville. Remember that all of your answers will remain completely confidential.

1. What is your age? [READ CHOICES]

     1   18-24
     2   25-34
     3   35-44
     4   45-54
     5   55-64
     6   65 and OVER

2. Which of the following best describes the highest level of formal education that you have completed? [READ CHOICES]

     1   LESS THAN HIGH SCHOOL
     2   HIGH SCHOOL GRADUATE
     3   SOME COLLEGE
     4   COLLEGE GRADUATE
     5   POSTGRADUATE OR PROFESSIONAL DEGREE

3. To indicate the part of town in which you reside, can you tell us the last **two** digits of your zip code?

     379____

4. How many people live in your household, including yourself? [ENTER NUMBER]

     _____

5. How many children under 18 reside in your household?   [ENTER NUMBER]

     _____

6. What is your race? Are you black, white, or some other race?   [CIRCLE NUMBER]

     1   BLACK
     2   WHITE
     3   OTHER

7. Finally, which of the following categories best describes your total household income for 1997?
                                                                [READ CHOICES]
     1   Less than $15,000
     2   $15,000 - $24,999
     3   $25,000 - $34,999
     4   $35,000 - $49,999
     5   $50,000 - $74,999
     6   $75,000 - $99,999
     7   $100,000 or more

Figure 2.4. Examples of Attribute and Background Questions

Specifying Information Needs

To accomplish all of a survey's objectives, it is useful for the designer to specify precisely what type of information is needed. Is it an attitude, belief, or behavior that decision makers want to know more about? Are there specific groups in the population who are likely to have widely disparate perspectives on an issue and, if so, why? What background questions will identify these groups? Are several questions necessary to measure the complexity or diversity of respondents' opinions, attitudes, experiences, or behaviors?

Anticipating what decision makers need to know requires substantive knowledge about the topics being investigated and some familiarity with previous research findings on the topic(s) of interest. Knowledge acquired through experience, research, and interviews with representatives of various groups, interests, and agencies with a stake in the findings of the survey is integral to an "environmental scanning" process. The fruit of this process will be an intelligently designed, parsimonious questionnaire containing the number and types of questions that will satisfy the project's information objectives.

If policy makers need to know, for instance, what citizens of a particular state think about a new health care financing system, it behooves the survey researcher to learn how the program is supposed to work and what impacts or effects are claimed by both its supporters and its detractors. This environmental scanning process yields dividends when it comes time for the researcher to compose the right kinds of questions that will adequately plumb people's opinions, attitudes, and experiences. It is also essential that the researcher be sure to include important screen or attribute questions that will enable policy makers to distinguish, for instance, among the important SES, occupational, and health status characteristics of respondents. Once there is agreement on the types of information needed, the researcher can focus on specific question wording.

Slight wording variations can often produce vastly different responses to attitude questions. Babbie (1995) describes how disparate opinions have been elicited when questioners have substituted specific terms, such as "welfare" for "assistance to the poor," "dealing with drug addiction" for "drug rehabilitation," "improving conditions of blacks" for "assistance to blacks," and "halting the rising crime rate" for "law enforcement" (p. 146). Depending upon which description was used, programs in each instance received substantially different levels of public support. In one survey, for example, a 68.2% majority thought that too little money was being spent on "assistance to the poor," whereas in another matched survey in the same year, only 23.1% thought that too little money was being spent on "welfare." The point is that the survey designer should always be clear on the objective of a question, the type of information it seeks to elicit, and how the use of loaded or biased terms can result in a very different response distribution.

A general rule of good survey design is to specify the type of information needed and then to draft a question that measures the concept of interest without evoking some visceral reaction to a particular term. The question designer should always try to imagine how he or she would answer a particular question. As Babbie (1995) plainly puts it: "If you'd feel embarrassed, perverted, inhumane, stupid, irresponsible, or anything like that, you should give some serious thought to whether others" will feel likewise (p. 146). If complex concepts or controversial issues are involved, several questions may be required to obtain valid measures of all of the important dimensions of that opinion, attitude, belief, perception, or behavior. Pretests will help to detect any problems in a question's clarity or meaning.

FOCUS GROUPS

Often, the researcher is unable to anticipate everything citizens think is important about an issue or service. When unable to specify in advance everything that should be included in a questionnaire, the researcher may want to hold one or more focus groups to help identify and explore unanticipated concerns, thoughts, and reactions in the population. Frank discussions among small groups of 8 to 10 representative members of the population, led by a moderator who keeps the group focused on a particular topic, can be a productive source of ideas for later questionnaire items as well as an initial pretest forum for draft questions (Morgan, 1993). Open-ended questions asked in this type of setting, for instance, can be the basis for the development of good response sets for closed-ended items. A focus group includes too few individuals to be considered a valid representation of the opinions of the larger population, but the comments expressed and the reactions observed among participants can help researchers to avoid many sins of omission or commission in deciding what questions to include and how to ask them.

Frank and probing discussions, creativity, and spontaneity characterize good focus group sessions. A skilled moderator encourages participants to discuss their thoughts, feelings, and reactions openly. Focus group sessions can provide insight into how some people in the population think about various topics. This information is especially useful when the purpose of the survey is to explore issues or concerns that are not widely known or well understood. The researcher should expect to pay a small stipend to each focus group participant to entice people to attend a 1- to 2-hour evening session. The value of such meetings usually exceeds their cost because understanding how customers view things will help the researcher to design a valid, sensitive instrument.

THE TIME DIMENSION

Time is an important dimension in the planning of the survey project. *When* survey results are needed will affect the decision about the type of contact method, an aspect of time discussed later in this chapter. Another consideration is whether the survey is a one-shot deal or part of a continuing process of policy planning or service evaluation. A *cross-sectional* survey examines a population at one particular point in time; it is essentially a one-time snapshot of what a population thinks or believes at the time the questions are asked. This kind of survey is especially well suited for exploratory and descriptive information objectives. A *longitudinal* survey collects observations for a population on more than one occasion. Its chief purpose is to measure change and to identify trends in behaviors, attitudes, and perceptions. Such information is particularly useful for evaluation studies that track performance and indicate whether a program, service, or team is doing what it is supposed to do for citizens, clients, or customers.

The primary research design distinction between cross-sectional and longitudinal surveys is that longitudinal studies must ask precisely the same questions each time they are administered, so that change in any variable can be tracked. New questions and variables can be included, but conclusions about how opinions or characteristics change over time are possible only for items worded identically from survey to survey. If it is possible that a survey will be part of a longitudinal research effort, the designer should take extra care in question wording to anticipate the kinds of information that will be useful to decision makers in the future.

In addition, the researcher has at least three options in selecting the type of sample to use in a longitudinal survey. A *trend* study draws different samples from the same general population at different times. The population may include all persons in a country, a state, a city, a neighborhood, or a research methods class, but different persons respond each time the survey is administered. When there is a need to track a specific kind of group in a population, a *cohort* study is appropriate. A cohort can be any group with definable attributes whose members can be located and contacted over time. A cohort study, for example, might include all city voters registered in 1994, all persons who received an M.P.A. degree during the 1990-1995 period, or all persons who practice composting in their backyards. Different persons respond in each of the surveys, but all share membership in the defining cohort group. When it is important to examine change in the *very same cases* in a population over time, a *panel* survey is appropriate. This type of survey tracks the same people who participated in the first survey in successive surveys. In other words, the exact same sample is used over time. If 450 cities with recycling programs in 1996 constitute the original sample, then the same 450 cities receive questionnaires in any subsequent study. A panel survey is unique in that it permits the researcher to measure the precise effects of some stimuli or policy decision for individuals or groups of matched cases. One disadvantage of this type of longitudinal study is mortality; that is, subjects may drop out for various reasons, and that can affect the representativeness of the sample.

Most survey projects are cross-sectional, one-time events. Increasingly, however, government initiatives in total quality management and customer satisfaction require a process for tracking opinions over time. By identifying trends, longitudinal studies vastly improve the measurement of performance and the ability of authorities to take actions to improve customer satisfaction. The sponsors of any given survey need to decide whether the project will be a one-time event or part of a continuing effort to obtain feedback.

Identifying the Target Population

Asking the right people is as important as asking the right questions in any survey. The *target population* consists of the individuals, households, or groups in the jurisdiction of interest. It can be any group or organization for which geographic, membership, or time referents can be defined. Who or what is being studied is called the *unit of analysis*. The units in the target population could be all users of the city park facilities or all environmental groups whose members testify at congressional hearings on regulation of the nuclear industry. The target population is what the researcher wants to make generalizations about. The unit of analysis is the object about which information is collected.

Clear focus on the unit of analysis is important to avoid an *ecological fallacy*. This occurs, for example, when inferences about individuals are drawn from data measuring some other unit of analysis, such as a census district or a neighborhood. Suppose, for example, that more recyclable newsprint is collected at drop-off centers located in census tracts where the populations have higher median educational attainment and higher mean incomes than in other tracts. Fewer tons are collected in census tracts where the citizens have fewer median years of formal schooling and lower mean incomes. A researcher commits an ecological fallacy if he or she concludes from this information that citizens with more formal education and higher incomes recycle more newsprint. Because the study is based only on aggregate information about the population in census tracts, it is impossible to know precisely *who* recycles how much newsprint. Other factors may account for variations in how much newsprint is recycled. One can draw conclusions only about the unit of analysis for which the data are collected.

Avoiding ecological fallacies seems simple enough in surveys that typically have individuals as the unit of analysis, but, as Miller and Miller (1991) point out, "one of the most common mistakes made in citizen surveys is asking the wrong people the right questions" (p. 31). What this means is that questions should be asked only of the individuals who are likely to have some knowledge, exposure, or experience with the topic, service, or issue of interest. The respondent must be qualified to answer the question posed. Asking all county citizens what they think about the new curriculum in the public schools will result in a high proportion of "don't know" or "no opinion" responses, because only parents who take active interest in their children's education are likely to know anything about the new curriculum. Conversely, there are some issues on which most citizens have informed opinions, such as neighborhood safety.

In planning a survey, it is critical for the designer to distinguish between questions on which everyone has an opinion and those that should be answered only by recipients or users of a particular service or program. Once again, screen questions are helpful because they ensure that questions are directed to the respondents who say they have some knowledge about or experience with particular items. On a mail questionnaire, screen questions usually have arrows leading from them to direct respondents to the questions they should answer next; on questionnaires used by telephone interviewers, special instructions tell the interviewer what questions to ask, depending on respondents' answers to the screen questions.

Which questions should be directed to all respondents and which should be asked only of particular groups in the population? Most citizens know something about the services and programs that are part of everyday life experiences, such as those related to taxation, transportation, solid waste collection, recreational and cultural facilities, water quality, health care, housing, shopping, personal security issues (police and fire protection), employment opportunities, quality of life, and schools. Other services and programs are community or neighborhood specific, and it may be necessary to include screen questions on these topics.

Screen questions extend the completion time for a questionnaire, which increases the "cost" to respondents of participating in the survey. It is important for the designer to strive for a balance between the overall length of the survey and the number of questions directed to specific groups. The use of many screen questions can also increase the monetary cost of a survey, because a larger sample of the population may have to be drawn to reach the number of individuals needed for the researcher to have confidence in the accuracy of any generalizations drawn from respondents' opinions. The more selective the screens, the more phone calls (or mailings) will be required to reach the intended target population.

Precise definition of the target population also is important because of the practical considerations of drawing a sample. The investigator will identify and select the cases (individuals, households, or group members) in the target population that constitute a *sampling frame,* or the operational definition of the population that provides the basis for sampling. A sampling frame may be a listing of all cases in the target population or the cases that satisfy certain membership criteria. In a mail survey, for example, an address list of all city residents can be purchased from an address listing service; in such a case, the list constitutes the sampling frame. In a telephone survey, the sampling frame might consist of the city phone book, a computer file of all numbers connected to the 911 emergency service (a listing), or a set of telephone numbers within a particular telephone exchange (a "membership" criterion).

As I explain in Chapter 3, a list of all members of the target population often does not exist, so selection criteria must be created. Criteria for different sites, days, times, or seasons can be used to select the cases to be interviewed. As long as members of the population can be identified, it is usually possible for the researcher to define a reasonable selection procedure. Later problems can be avoided if the researcher considers during the planning stage how easy or difficult it will be to construct a sampling frame for the target population.

Methods of Contact: The Merits
of Mail, Telephone, and Face-to-Face Surveys

The choice to be made among mail, telephone, and face-to-face contact methods is an important part of the planning stage. Which contact method is best for a given survey depends on many different factors. All of the methods have advantages and disadvantages, and they may not apply equally, or perhaps at all, to every survey project. As Dillman (1978) notes, "Until the attributes of each method are considered in relation to the study topic, the population to be surveyed, and the precise survey objectives, the question of which is best cannot be answered" (p. 39). The researcher's selection of a survey method should be guided by one main consideration: how to design the best possible survey that accomplishes the purposes of the study within the limitations imposed by time, money, personnel, equipment, and other resource constraints. In this context, the best survey is one that is as accurate as possible.

Accuracy is the touchstone of survey quality. An accurate survey is one in which the respondents and the opinion distributions are representative of the larger target population. Survey sponsors are always interested in keeping costs low, but there is an inherent trade-off between cost and accuracy when it comes to the size of the sample. If resources permit only a very small sample size, the chances that the results may not accurately represent the larger population are increased. If the results cannot be generalized to the target population within an acceptable level of confidence and margin of error, then the survey's value is diminished considerably. Whatever citizen survey method a researcher selects, he or she should strive to attain the maximum possible accuracy within the time and resource constraints that exist. Chapter 3 discusses how researchers can calculate sample size so they can have a certain confidence that the results represent the larger population within a tolerable error margin.

Table 2.2 rates the three major survey methods on several dimensions, including cost, personnel requirements, implementation time, and accuracy. Miller and Miller (1991) report that 43% of cities use mail surveys, 40% use telephone surveys, and only 3% conduct face-to-face interviews; another 6% use some combination of methods. Mail surveys are probably the least expensive of the three kinds to conduct. Phone interviews represent the quickest way to complete a survey and are also relatively inexpensive if toll charges can be avoided. Personal interviews constitute the most costly method, but they may yield the richest data about the topics of interest. No survey method is poor—there are only poorly crafted and badly executed survey instruments. Each method has strengths and weaknesses that arise in the context of the purpose of the survey, the population surveyed, and the kinds of information needed to fulfill the study's objectives. The considerations discussed here have relevance in the context of these factors.

TABLE 2.2 Relative Merits and Rankings of Mail, Telephone, and Face-to-Face Surveys on Selected Criteria

Criterion	Mail	Telephone	Face-to-Face
Data collection cost	low (1)	low to mod. (2)	high (3)
Personnel required	few (1)	several (2)	many (3)
Implementation time	long (2)	short (1)	long (3)
Importance of accurate population list	high (3)	low (1)	high (3)
Control over respondent selection	low (3)	mod. to high (2)	high (1)
Response rate	low to mod. (3)	high (1)	mod. to high (2)
Control over interviewer bias and error	high (1)	moderate (2)	low to mod. (3)
Length of the questionnaire	short to mod. (3)	moderate (2)	mod. to long (1)
Capacity to handle complex questions	moderate (2)	low to mod. (3)	mod. to high (1)
Response to open-ended questions	low to mod. (3)	moderate (2)	mod. to high (1)
Completion of longer, tedious questions	low (3)	moderate (2)	mod. to high (1)
Completion of sensitive questions	moderate (2)	mod. to high (1)	low to mod. (3)
Perceived confidentiality of responses	low to mod. (2)	mod. to high (1)	low (3)
Probability respondent will skip questions	high (3)	low (1)	low (1)
Mean performance ranking	2.29	1.64	2.07

NOTE: 1 = most satisfactory; 2 = satisfactory; 3 = least satisfactory.

COST CONSIDERATIONS

Frey (1989) identifies three important elements to consider in calculating and comparing the costs of different survey methods: sample size, geographic dispersion of the sample, and the length of the interview or questionnaire. Variations in wage rates, telephone charges, supply prices, costs of professional services, and sampling expenses can also account for price differentials, but, in general, costs increase as the sample size, geographic dispersion of the sample, and length of the interview or questionnaire increase.

Larger samples require more postage and supplies for a mail survey and more hours of interviewing for telephone and face-to-face surveys. Geographically dispersed samples drive up the costs for both personal and telephone surveys. It is more expensive to get interviewers to and from sites spread out over a wide area, and making return trips to interview respondents who were previously unavailable adds considerably to the project budget. For telephone surveys, costs increase when interviews must be conducted with individuals outside the local calling area. Dispersion and distance factors do not substantially affect the costs of mail surveys, self-administered surveys, or telephone surveys that are limited to phone numbers within a local calling area.

Interview or questionnaire length has a substantial effect on survey costs. For mail surveys, printing and postage costs vary with the number of pages and the weight of the questionnaire packet to be mailed. These costs increase if the instrument exceeds 12 page faces, a cover letter, and a return postage-paid envelope. Three folded 8½-by-11-inch sheets with two staples in the spine create a 5½-by-8½-inch booklet, and three folded 8½-by-17-inch sheets create an 8½-by-8½-inch booklet.

Time is money. As interview length increases, so do personnel costs for both face-to-face and telephone surveys. Longer interviews require more stamina on the part of callers, and they risk a higher rate of premature termination by fatigued respondents. Question structure also affects the time it takes to complete an interview. Open-ended questions require more time and effort for respondents, who must think about the questions and then recall and phrase their responses. Not surprisingly, this is why many people skip such questions or decide not to respond at all. In turn, with low response rates, postage costs increase because of the need to send a larger number of follow-up mailings.

In cost comparisons of methods, the advantage usually goes to mail surveys. They are the least expensive to administer to a dispersed population because of standardized postage rates, and they require less labor than do the other methods. Printing costs can be minimized if the survey researcher has access to a word processor, a laser printer, and a high-quality photocopier that can make two-sided copies. The itemized costs of the mail survey include postage, paper, envelopes, supplies, and labor. Survey staff prepare the questionnaire booklet, use the mail-merge function of a word processing program to print cover letters and address labels, and stuff envelopes. A good rule of thumb for researchers to use in budgeting for follow-up mailings is to double the cost of the original mailing; this amount should cover the costs of two or three subsequent attempts to reach non-respondents. The use of business reply-type return envelopes minimizes postage costs, but adds some marginal expense to printing costs. With such return envelopes, the survey researcher's account with the local post office incurs charges only for the questionnaires actually returned; also, these envelopes remove some respondents' temptation to peel off the stamp and toss the survey.

Personal interviews are the most expensive of the three kinds of contact methods, which helps to explain why so few organizations conduct such interviews. Depending upon the size and geographic distribution of the sample, projects involving personal interviews may cost two to three times more per completed questionnaire than telephone surveys. The major financial considerations in surveys using personal interviews are the costs of training, supervision, travel, and labor. Safety and security are also core concerns for both the interviewer and potential respondents. In most areas of the United States, many people will not open their doors to strangers. Furthermore, sending interviewers out into the field can expose a public organization to additional liability risks—for example, if an employee or volunteer is injured or harmed in the course of interviewer duties. The difficulties involved in reaching the appropriate people with whom to conduct personal interviews increase project completion time and costs.

Telephone survey costs usually fall somewhere between those for mail and face-to-face surveys. A sample of 600 numbers in a local calling area, for instance, may cost about $10.00 per completed 10-minute interview if callers are paid about $6.00 an hour. Costs increase with the length of the survey, the need to screen for certain types or groups of respondents, prevailing personnel costs, and the time it takes to supervise and train the callers. Using in-house volunteers to make calls is one way to reduce costs and avoid the fees charged by professional polling firms.

PERSONNEL REQUIREMENTS

Few personnel are needed to conduct a mail survey. Clerical employees can stuff envelopes according to instructions, track mailings, record returns, and send out follow-up mailings. Preparation of the survey instrument, the cover letter, and procedures for follow-up mailings are the responsibility of the survey researcher. Mail surveys are less labor-intensive than either face-to-face or telephone surveys.

Telephone interviewers must be trained properly and must have reasonable social skills, so that they can persuade people to participate, follow instructions precisely, and get through items in a long list without breaking the rhythm of the interview. The demands on the supervisors of telephone interviewers are even greater: They must be able to monitor the team of interviewers and resolve problems and questions quickly.

Conducting a survey using face-to-face interviews generally requires a team of 8 to 10 interviewers, depending on the geographic area to be covered and time constraints. Members of the survey crew must have the social skills to establish almost instant rapport with respondents and must be able to work weekends and evenings. They must be trained more extensively than telephone interviewers because they may encounter a variety of situations in the field that will require independent decision making. Occasionally, the supervisor may need to accompany an interviewer to deal with a difficult situation or problem that has arisen. For all these reasons, labor costs are highest for face-to-face interviews.

IMPLEMENTATION TIME

A well-trained, experienced telephone interviewer should be able to complete about four 6-minute interviews per hour, depending upon contact and cooperation rates. During a 3-hour calling session, eight well-trained and experienced callers may complete about 96 calls. An eight-person team can complete calls to 600 households in about 19 hours. Normally, calling hours are spread over a 3- to 4-day period, to allow time to complete all required callbacks.

Telephone surveys have the distinct advantage of producing swift results. Responses can be entered in a data file while other calls are being completed. Computer-assisted telephone interviewing (CATI) software, discussed in Chapter 5, accelerates the process even more by creating the data file as responses are entered at the keyboard by the caller. With this technology, it is possible for a telephone survey project to be completed virtually overnight.

Personal interview and mail surveys usually require the longest time to complete. Recruiting and training personnel, locating respondents, and making follow-up visits to nonrespondents increase the time and costs of surveys involving personal interviews. Likewise, it is not uncommon for mail surveys to take 6 to 8 weeks to complete. The objective of both methods is to obtain an acceptable response rate, which may require two or more follow-up visits or mailings per nonresponding individual.

ACCURACY

A survey is accurate to the extent that the responses are representative of the larger population. Not every citizen or household in a random sample will return a mail questionnaire or consent to be interviewed. The researcher's objective is to get the *highest possible* response rate, because the higher the response rate, the more likely it is that the survey responses represent the population accurately. The response rate is the number of completions compared with the number of eligible persons in the sample. Tremendous effort is invested in decisions about the type, order, wording, and number of questions, the appearance of the instrument, the interviewer instructions, and assurances of confidentiality associated with the survey because all of these factors affect the final response rate.

The three contact methods typically have different response rates, with telephone interviews usually having the highest rates. Well-trained telephone interviewers can establish rapport with prospective respondents and plead for their voluntary participation. Telephone interviews are also safer for the caller and less threatening to respondents than the stranger who knocks on the door.

Generally, refusal rates are on the rise for all types of surveys. Several factors affect refusals to participate, foremost among which are the fear of opening the door to a stranger and fear of being inundated by survey requests that lack any perceived relevance to real life. The replacement techniques discussed in Chapter 3 enable the researcher to attain 100% of the desired sample size for a telephone survey. A well-designed mail survey can usually net a response rate between 50% and 60%. Any response rate greater than 70% is considered excellent for a mail survey. Outstanding response rates for personal interview projects range from 60% to 70%.

Dealing With Nonresponses

Do nonresponses bias survey results? A dilemma that cannot always be resolved satisfactorily is how to determine whether the people who choose not to respond to a mail or personal interview survey differ much from those who do respond, other than being less cooperative or willing to participate. The higher the refusal rate, the more important it is for the researcher to determine whether refusals bias the results.

The scholarly literature suggests that respondents and nonrespondents often have similar opinions about most local government services and programs. In my experience, nonrespondents to mail and telephone surveys tend to be male, be members of ethnic minorities, and have lower levels of formal education than do respondents. Conversely, those with higher levels of education and those who feel relatively strongly about issues are more likely to respond. In the interests of accuracy, the researcher should strive to avoid this potential source of bias and to determine whether any opinion differences exist between respondents and nonrespondents.

Several strategies can be used to assess possible nonresponse bias. First, are the nonresponses concentrated in any particular group or area? By comparing the demographics of the incoming responses with the most recent census data for the target population, the researcher may be able to ascertain the representativeness of the responding population. The value of including appropriate attribute questions is once again evident here. The potential for bias exists whenever the attribute variables in the survey differ from the recent census data on gender, race, income, education, home-ownership, age, employment status, or census tract by more than a few percentage points.

The researcher may also find it useful to examine the distributions on various opinions, attitudes, behaviors, and beliefs among whites and blacks, the rich and the poor, males and females, or any other demographic factor of interest that appears to be underrepresented. Nonresponses among a particular group are tolerable if there are no large differences (more than a few percentage points) in how the different groups rate, evaluate, or think about the important dependent concepts in the survey. If large opinion differences occur between different groups, those underrepresented may have to be sampled separately, or the results may be statistically weighted following the guidelines in Chapter 3.

Strategies for Surveying
Elite or Specialized Populations

There are occasions when public administrators need to study relatively small, select groups of individuals. These may comprise, for example, members of the local chamber of commerce, federal managers in charge of conducting public hearings for a nuclear waste repository, leaders of state civil rights groups, or coordinators of local nonprofit social service organizations. The feature common to all such groups is that the use of a highly structured and standardized questionnaire format usually will not work very well.

There are several reasons standardized questionnaires are often inappropriate for use with small, specialized populations. Foremost among these is that the researcher may not know enough about the subject or problem of interest to create a standard list of questions. The group members may be the only ones with the expertise to frame the nature of the problem or issue of interest accurately. The purpose of the research may be to explore or to improve understanding of a viewpoint, perception, opinion, or situation that is too complex to be described adequately by a set of mutually exclusive categories. As both students and practitioners of public administration know, there are some questions for which essays are the most appropriate responses. A related point is that attempts to inquire about a complex issue or problem by creating a battery of questions about it usually result in questionnaires that have too many open-ended questions, which can frustrate even the most patient participants. In such cases, to obtain an acceptable quality and quantity of responses, researchers need to conduct semistructured or focused personal interviews.

Interviewers require special preparation to conduct successful personal interviews with "elites," defined by Lewis Dexter (1970), author of the classic text in this field, as anyone "given special, non-standardized treatment" (p. 5) to elicit information. The nonstandardized treatment to which Dexter refers includes situations in which the interviewee's definition of the situation is stressed; the interviewee is encouraged to structure the account of some situation; or the interviewee is prompted to describe the problem, the question, or notions of what is relevant.

The interviewer should address several logistical and methodological issues before attempting to conduct such *specialized* interviews (the preferred term, as *elite* connotes superiority); the process is not as simple as "lining up a few interviews and chatting for a while" (Johnson & Joslyn, 1991, p. 193). First, it is important that the interviewer prepare as fully as possible for the interviews by researching and learning everything he or she can about the topic to be discussed. With such background knowledge, the interviewer can frame reasonably intelligent questions about the aspects of the topic that he or she wants group members to comment or elaborate upon. This preparation will also help the interviewer to recognize the need to follow up on certain responses with probe questions. If nothing else, the interviewer's being well prepared will impress interviewees with the interviewer's serious interest in the topic (Johnson & Joslyn, 1991).

The product of the interviewer's preparation should be an *interview guide* that orders the topics and questions to be discussed. The specificity of this guide will depend on how much topical control the interviewer desires. The interviewer may consider telling busy prospective interviewees on the phone beforehand what he or she wants to know, so that they can collect any data about the subject prior to the meeting. Alternatively, the interviewer might write to each individual and enumerate the project's objectives and the kinds of information the interviewer would like to obtain.

During the specialized interview, the researcher must "listen, observe, think, and take notes" while maintaining a good rapport with the respondent (Johnson & Joslyn, 1991, p. 195). Accomplishing all these tasks simultaneously is a challenge for the best of interviewers, so it is a good idea to ask permission of the respondent to use a tape recorder, so the interviewer can focus during the interview on listening and comprehending. Later, the researcher's main methodological challenge is to summarize and categorize the interviewee's responses. If the responses have been frank and truthful, usually the researcher can discern from them some pattern or plausible set of generalizations.

Summary

Planning is the most critical stage of the survey research process, because the decisions reached at this stage affect the quality of the entire enterprise. The researcher and survey sponsors should reach consensus on the sponsors' basic information needs and the objectives of the survey and whether the kind of information needed can be obtained best through a cross-sectional or a longitudinal study.

The study's sponsors should be aware of the kinds of information that surveys can reasonably be expected to measure. At the outset, the researcher must identify the target population, specify the unit of analysis, and decide which method is best for questioning the members of the target population. What to ask, who to ask, and how to ensure that the results accurately represent the population are decisions that should be guided by the study's objectives and by the sampling principles described in the next chapter.

The researcher must budget sufficient resources for the survey to attain the levels of accuracy and reliability desired. Resolution of these issues in the planning stage dramatically improves the value of the survey findings for decision makers.

3

Sampling

The selection of cases from the target population follows the decisions made by the researcher about information needs, survey objectives, the target population, the unit of analysis, and the method of contact. When resources are sufficient to send everyone in the target population a questionnaire, there is no need to draw a sample. Relatively small populations, such as the population of registered state lobbyists or members of the Capitol Hill press corps, may consist of only a few hundred or a score of individuals. Data gathered from an entire population are more accurate than data gathered from a sample, which will always have some error in approximations of population parameters. Researchers whose projects are small enough that they can survey entire populations may want to scan this chapter briefly and then move on to the instrument design guidelines described in Chapter 4. For those whose projects, because of necessity or for convenience, require a sample, this chapter illustrates selection methods that meet the standards of good social science.

Sampling is the science of selecting cases in a way that enables the researcher to make accurate inferences about a larger population. The two primary decisions in the sampling stage concern sample size and the method for selecting a probability sample. These decisions are governed by information needs, the desired level of confidence and precision, and available resources.

The Logic of Sampling

As noted above, sampling is unnecessary if the population to be surveyed is small. Everyone in a 15-member group, for instance, can be asked questions directly. For larger populations, researchers must select samples in *unbiased* ways to ensure that no group or stratum is systematically over- or underrepresented. To accomplish this, they must employ the methods of *probability sampling*. Through the process of random selection, a researcher selects a subset of the larger population that enables him or her to know with a certain level of confidence and a certain margin of error what people in the entire target population think. The selection procedures described in this chapter will help public administrators to obtain probability samples that are the most efficient size to accomplish the objectives of their survey projects.

The sampling stage of the survey research process is so vital that the usefulness and quality of the survey's results depend on how well it is accomplished. Figure 3.1 lists the key elements of the sample selection process.

A *representative sample* is one that has every major attribute of the larger population present in about the same proportions. If 47% of the population is male, then about the same proportion of the sample should be male. If 63% of the entire population favors a balanced budget amendment, the sample results should approximate this proportion. How can researchers know whether a sample is representative of a particular population if they know nothing about the population's characteristics or about the opinions of its members? The answer is that they can never know *for sure* that their sample *exactly* mirrors the population. However, if they apply the principles of probability theory, researchers can *estimate* their sample's accuracy and establish a certain level of confidence in their estimate. In practice, researchers can be quite confident on the basis of only a very small fraction of sample cases, if these cases are selected randomly.

A sample represents an estimate of various *population parameters,* or characteristics that interest the researcher. The parameters of interest may be demographic features or particular opinions, beliefs, or behaviors. An

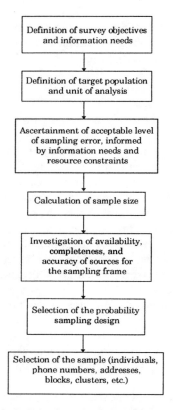

Figure 3.1. Key Elements in Selecting a Probability Sample

example is the proportion of citizens who favor a balanced budget amendment. A sample's estimate of a population characteristic is called a *statistic.* Because *any* estimate, by its very nature, is likely to be imperfect, there is always the possibility of some error. The difference between a sample statistic and the actual population parameter is known as *sampling error.* Because all samples are estimates, they all have some margin of sampling error. Sample statistics may underestimate or overestimate actual population parameters; seldom are they perfectly representative of a population—this is the price that researchers must pay for reducing the costs of measuring popular opinions.

Just how much sampling error should be tolerated? This judgment depends partly on the purposes of the survey and how much money is available. Money is an issue because it costs more to increase the size of the sample, and this is one way to reduce sampling error and improve accuracy. In a close election race, for example, a smart candidate is likely to want highly accurate survey results, because a margin of error of ±3% will not help to detect small shifts in opinion that might suggest whether the final advertising blitz is having the desired effect. On the other hand, managers who use surveys of customer satisfaction to compare the performance of service teams over time may accept a larger margin of error, perhaps plus or minus 4 or 5 percentage points, in an estimate of the proportion of customers who are "very satisfied."

Statisticians call this margin or range of error a *confidence interval.* It is measured in units called *standard error.* The size of the standard error is the basis for measuring the accuracy of the estimates in the sample. In other words, it measures the extent to which the sample estimates are distributed around the population parameter. If 65% of the respondents in the sample are "very satisfied" with a service and the margin of error is ±4%, then the sample result provides an estimate that between 61% and 69% of the target population is very satisfied with the service.

In addition to the margin of error, another important aspect of sample accuracy is the *level of confidence,* or how sure we can be that a particular sample's estimates fall within a specified range of a statistic. The only way to be 100% certain about a population parameter is to ask everyone in the population, but because this is often impractical, researchers settle for being somewhat less than absolutely sure. Most public administrators will accept a confidence level of 95% or 99%. This means that if we were to draw 100 separate samples of a population, the sample's estimates of the population parameters would fall within a designated range of acceptable error in 95 (or 99) of the 100 samples. If the sample is a certain size, we can say that we are 95% sure that between 61% and 69% of the population are "very satisfied" with the service. Of course, there is a 5% chance that the actual population parameter falls outside this range, but most researchers are willing to accept these odds.

The information needs of the survey and the resources available to select a larger sample size govern the level of acceptable risk that a sample incorrectly estimates a population's parameters. Ideally, the margin of error should be small and the confidence level high. Together, the margin of error and the confidence level constitute sampling error (Johnson & Joslyn, 1991), which is expressed in how the results of a sample survey are described. For example, we might be 95% sure, with an error margin of ±2 percentage points, that 55% of the voters in Springfield will support Ms. Goodfellow in the next mayoral election.

The distinct advantage of a probability sample is that the researcher can attain a high level of confidence and a small range of error without having to draw a huge proportion of cases from the population. Based on probability theory, *samples of a certain size are likely to be representative of the population from which they are selected if all members of that population have a nonzero and an equal or known chance of being included in the sample.* It is this basic principle of probability sampling that enables researchers to make legitimate use of statistical inference and to calculate precisely the sampling error, or the chances that a sample of a certain size will be representative of a population within a specified range of error.

Clearly, the two important considerations in this principle are sample size and sample selection. Sample size is sometimes referred to as the *sampling fraction,* or the percentage of the entire population selected for the sample. The next section examines how to determine sample sizes for surveys with different levels of confidence and accuracy. Later in the chapter, I review the ways to incorporate random selection in choosing cases for a probability sample so that the confidence and accuracy standards set by the researcher actually can be achieved.

Determining Sample Size

How large does a probability sample need to be? An "efficient" sample is just large enough to be representative of the population (or its subgroups) at the confidence level and degree of accuracy desired by the researcher. The primary factors that affect sample size are the desired levels of accuracy and confidence, the heterogeneity of the population, and, to a much lesser extent, the size of the population. The higher the levels of accuracy and confidence desired, the larger the samples required. Great diversity within a population and a desire to analyze or compare subgroups in a population also make larger samples necessary.

To understand what it means to select a particular confidence level and margin of error for a sample, we need to examine more closely the logic of probability theory. Probability theory tells us that if we were to take many samples of a population, which of course no one has the time to do, the statistics from those samples would be distributed around an actual population parameter in a known way. In fact, they would resemble a bell-shaped or normal curve. Most sample estimates would cluster in the middle of the bell and fewer near the edges or tails of the bell curve. Furthermore, probability theory tells us that a certain proportion of all samples will have estimates that fall within a certain distance of the actual population parameter. This distance is measured in standard errors.

CONFIDENCE LEVELS AND INTERVALS

Probability theory dictates that if we draw a large number of samples of a population, 95% of them will have estimates that fall within 1.96 standard errors (plus or minus) of the population's true parameters. Only 5% will have estimates that lie outside this range. In 99% of all samples, the estimates will fall within ± 2.58 standard errors of the true population parameter. Of course, researchers select just one sample, but, as Babbie (1995) explains, "knowing what it would be like to select thousands of samples allows us to make assumptions about the one we do select and study" (p. 202). Researchers rely on this logic of probability theory to make inferences about larger populations based on just one sample.

To apply this theory, we establish a level of confidence that our sample's estimates are within a certain number of standard errors of the actual population parameter. We can be 95% confident that they lie within 1.96 standard errors, or 99% confident that they lie within 2.58 standard errors, of the actual population parameter. If we want to be almost positive (99.9% sure), we can accept sample estimates that lie within 3 standard errors of the actual value in the population. Clearly, as confidence increases, the margin of error is larger.

In practice, researchers want to be highly confident in the accuracy of their results. The accuracy of any *particular* sample is a function of two things: the size of the sample and the actual population parameter. The neat thing about the formula for the standard error is that it indicates how closely the estimates of a sample of any size are clustered around an actual population parameter, even when the true value of the population is unknown. With this formula, we establish for a sample of any size how confident we are that its estimates lie within a certain margin of error (accuracy) of the population's parameter, *regardless* of the size of that population.

A practical example illustrates this logic. Suppose the budget department chief is charged with investigating public support for a proposed school bond issue. She figures that there is enough money in the special projects account to conduct about 400 telephone interviews. If a sample of this size is selected, how accurately will it estimate the population's opinion on this controversial issue, and what confidence can the budget chief have in her findings? To answer these questions, she calculates the formula for the standard error of a sample:

$$SE = \sqrt{p\,(1-p\,)/n}\ ,$$

where p is the proportion of the population that actually supports (or opposes) the school bond issue and n is the sample size.

Obviously, no one really knows what proportion really supports or opposes the bond issue. If we knew this, there would be no reason to conduct the survey. Our best guess, one that is the most conservative estimate of opinion variability or heterogeneity on any population parameter, is an even 50/50 (.5) split. Working the equation, we find the following:

$$SE = \sqrt{.5\,(\,1-.5\,)/400}\ ,$$
$$SE = \sqrt{.25/400}\ ,$$
$$SE = \sqrt{.025}\ .$$

Thus the standard error for these figures is .025, or 2.5%. The budget chief remembers her professor talking about the assumptions of probability theory and how she can be 95% sure that a sample's estimate will be within about 2 standard errors above or below the actual population opinion as long as the people interviewed are selected randomly from the population. For the problem at hand, 2 standard errors is equal to .05 or ±5% (2 × .025). Now she knows that she can be 95% confident that the error margin for the sample estimate will be ±5% of the actual proportion of the population that supports (or opposes) the school bond issue. Alternatively, with a sample of this size she can be 99.9% sure that the sample estimate will be within three standard errors above or below the actual population proportion that supports the bond issue. At this level of confidence, the margin of error is much broader, ±7.5% around the parameter. However, this hardly helps the budget chief to predict whether or not the school bond issue will pass.

The budget chief has reason to believe that the bond issue could be passed or defeated by a very narrow margin, if history is any guide. Accordingly, she decides that the sample's margin of error (confidence interval) has to be less than ±5%. To increase the precision of the findings, the standard error must be reduced. This requires a larger sample size. The square root in the standard error formula indicates that to cut the standard error in half, the sample size must be quadrupled. To reduce the standard error to .0125 (1.25%), a random sample of 1,600 (400 × 4) is necessary. With this sample size, the budget chief could be 95% confident that the sample estimate is within ±2.5% of the actual population's opinion. Because this sample size far exceeds her allotted budget, she decides to make the case to her supervisor for additional funds to achieve about a ± 3% error margin at the 95% confidence level. A sample size of about 1,100 satisfies this desired level of precision.

The trade-off between confidence level and precision is apparent in the sample size decision. The purpose of the survey and the resources available will ultimately govern the practical limits of a sample's size. For most administrative and managerial work, a confidence level of 95% and a margin of error of plus or minus 4 or 5 percentage points are satisfactory. The researcher must judge whether some incremental improvement in precision is worth the considerable additional cost.

O'Sullivan and Rassel (1995) point out the common misconception that "if the size of the population is larger, the sample size must be increased by a corresponding amount" (p. 134). The example above indicates that this is not so. Citizens occasionally find it intuitively difficult to believe that a sample size of 625 adults is sufficient to represent, with the *same* level of confidence and precision, the opinions of people in a city of 100,000 or in a state with a population of several million. It is best for researchers to be prepared to respond to this concern. A nonmathematical explanation is that as long as the population is relatively large, the proportion of the population sampled (the sampling fraction) does not have a big impact on precision, because it is the absolute *size of the sample* rather than the size of the sample fraction that determines precision. In mathematical terms, we can see that this is so because population size, per se, does not figure into the formula for calculating the standard error or accuracy of a sample.

SMALL POPULATIONS

For smaller populations, especially those of fewer than 120, sampling may not be any more convenient than selecting all of the cases in the population. If the dispersed nature of the small population requires the use of a sample, the researcher must add a population correction factor to the formula for computing the standard error of the sample, because the theoretical distribution of a smaller population does not resemble a normal curve. To estimate the standard error when sampling from small populations, we can employ the formula suggested by O'Sullivan and Rassel (1995, p. 147):

$$SE = \sqrt{p\,(\,1-p\,)/n} \times (\,N-n\,)/(\,N-1\,),$$

where p is the population proportion of interest, n is the sample size, and N is the population size. For a sample of 50 cases from a population of 100, assuming $p = .5$ for the population parameter of interest, the standard error is .035, or 3.5%. At the 95% level of confidence, the margin of error is ±7%.

ANALYSIS OF POPULATION SUBGROUPS

If the study aims to describe or compare the opinions, attitudes, or behaviors of various subgroups in the population, such as undecided voters or minority clients, then the researcher should consider the sampling error of the estimates of the parameters for these groups. A sample of 400 citizens, for example, has an overall sampling error of 5% at a 95% confidence level, but this sample size is not large enough to provide estimates at the *same* level of precision for a group that constitutes a much smaller proportion of the sample. The researcher must either accept a higher sampling error or select a larger sample of the subgroup from the population.

If, for example, a researcher wants to describe satisfaction with particular services among blacks, and if 15% of the population is black, then a population sample of 400 will have only about 60 blacks in it. In this case, estimates about the proportion of blacks who are satisfied or dissatisfied with the services have a standard error of 6.45% and an error range at the 95% confidence level of about ±13%. To attain a greater level of precision, the researcher must randomly select a larger sample of blacks. This type of disproportionate sampling can be incorporated into the sampling design. In effect, blacks would constitute a separate sample. Procedures for disproportionate sampling and the weighting of cases are discussed later in this chapter.

COMPUTING SAMPLE SIZE

How large does a sample need to be to attain a certain level of confidence and precision? For those who prefer to work the math themselves, instead of relying on tables that have already computed these numbers, the following example illustrates how to determine sample size for different levels of confidence and precision, depending on the project's purpose and budget.

In algebraic terms, the formula for determining the sample size is as follows:

$$\sqrt{n} = \sqrt{p\,(1-p)} \times (1.96\,)/a\,,$$

where n is the sample size, p is the population proportion of interest, 1.96 is the z score for the confidence level of 95% (it is 2.58 for 99% and 3.0 for 99.9%), and a is the level of accuracy desired.

If we want to be 95% confident that our sample estimates fall within ± 3% (.03) of the actual population's parameter, we compute sample size, n, as follows:

$$\sqrt{n} = \sqrt{(.5)(1-.5)} \times (1.96)/.03$$
$$= .5 \times 65.33 = 32.67$$
$$\sqrt{n} = 32.67$$
$$n = 32.67^2$$
$$n = 1{,}067.$$

Substituting an accuracy level of ± 4% results in a sample size of 600. If we want to be 99% sure that our sample estimates attain this level of accuracy, a sample size of 1,040 is required. Clearly, the researcher must judge whether some incremental improvement in confidence or precision is worth the additional cost.

The *quickest* way to obtain an estimate of sample size is simply to examine tables that have been prepared based on this equation and a population adjustment factor. Many researchers consult tables such as those reproduced here as Tables 3.1 and 3.2. Other sources that contain similar aids for determining sample size are O'Sullivan and Rassel (1995, p. 150) and Nachmias and Nachmias (1992, pp. 185-190). The figures in the two tables here offer conservative estimates of sample sizes for various populations at different levels of accuracy for the 95% and 99.7% confidence intervals, meaning that they assume maximum population variability (a 50/50 opinion split).

To use these tables, the researcher first decides whether to establish a 95% or 99.7% confidence interval for the population of interest. The columns indicate the desired margin of error. The sample size appropriate for the confidence and precision levels selected can be interpolated for populations that lie between the population sizes listed. For example, if we desire a 95% confidence level and a 3% error margin for a population of 22,500, the correct sample size is about 1,059, which is halfway between 1,053 and 1,064.

For smaller populations at specified confidence and error margins, the statistician who prepared these tables suggests using 50% of the population for the sample size. For populations of fewer than 500, when sampling is

TABLE 3.1 Sample Sizes for Specified Levels of Precision, 95%
Confidence Interval

Population	\pm 1\%	\pm 2\%	\pm 3\%	\pm 4\%	\pm 5\%
			Margin of Error		
500	*	*	*	*	222
1,000	*	*	*	385	286
1,500	*	*	638	441	316
2,000	*	*	714	476	333
2,500	*	1,250	769	500	345
3,000	*	1,364	811	517	353
3,500	*	1,485	843	530	359
4,000	*	1,538	870	541	364
4,500	*	1,607	891	549	367
5,000	*	1,667	909	556	370
6,000	*	1,765	938	566	375
7,000	*	1,842	959	574	378
8,000	*	1,905	976	580	381
9,000	*	1,957	989	584	383
10,000	5,000	2,000	1,000	588	385
15,000	6,000	2,143	1,034	600	390
20,000	6,667	2,222	1,053	606	392
25,000	7,143	2,273	1,064	610	394
50,000	8,333	2,381	1,087	617	397
100,000	9,091	2,439	1,099	621	398
100,000+	10,000	2,500	1,111	625	400

SOURCE: Yamane, Taro, *Elementary Sampling Theory,* © 1967, pp. 398-399. Adapted by permission of
Prentice Hall, Upper Saddle River, New Jersey.
*Sample size should be 50% of the population.

considered necessary, the small population correction factor can be used to
estimate the sample size for desired levels of confidence and precision.

Sampling Designs

Sampling design refers to how cases are selected from a *sampling frame.*
A sampling frame consists of the cases from which a probability sample is
selected. Singleton, Straits, and Straits (1993) identify two basic ways to create
a sampling frame: (a) list all the cases in the population, or (b) establish a
rule that defines membership in the population. Ideally, a sampling frame
contains all members of the target population, but in practice this goal is
difficult to achieve. Migration and other population changes make many

TABLE 3.2 Sample Sizes for Specified Levels of Precision, 99.7%
Confidence Interval

Population	Margin of Error				
	± 1%	± 2%	± 3%	± 4%	± 5%
500	*	*	*	*	*
1,000	*	*	*	*	474
1,500	*	*	*	726	563
2,000	*	*	*	826	621
2,500	*	*	*	900	662
3,000	*	*	1,364	958	692
3,500	*	*	1,458	1,003	716
4,000	*	*	1,539	1,041	735
4,500	*	*	1,607	1,071	750
5,000	*	*	1,667	1,098	763
6,000	*	2,903	1,765	1,139	783
7,000	*	3,119	1,842	1,171	798
8,000	*	3,303	1,905	1,196	809
9,000	*	3,462	1,957	1,216	818
10,000	*	3,600	2,000	1,233	826
15,000	*	4,091	2,143	1,286	849
20,000	*	4,390	2,222	1,314	861
25,000	11,842	4,592	2,273	1,331	869
50,000	15,517	5,056	2,381	1,368	884
100,000	18,367	5,325	2,439	1,387	892
100,000+	22,500	5,625	2,500	1,406	900

SOURCE: Yamane, Taro, *Elementary Sampling Theory,* © 1967, pp. 398-399. Adapted by permission of
Prentice Hall, Upper Saddle River, New Jersey.
*Sample size should be 50% of the population.

lists, such as telephone directories, outdated shortly after or even before
they are published. In the case of phone directories, unlisted numbers also
make them incomplete. This is why such directories are often called "dirty
lists." For these reasons, a full listing of a population is not always possible
or desirable. Many kinds of lists may be more accurate than telephone
directories, depending on the population of interest. The list of emergency
911 hookups, utility service lists, annual membership rosters and directories of various types, and property ownership records may yield more
accurate sampling frames for some populations. Current lists of residents
for some jurisdictions also can be purchased from mailing list companies.

Decision criteria for identifying and selecting cases from a population
may circumvent problems with inaccurate or incomplete population lists.
As Singleton et al. (1993) note, "As long as the cases can be identified, a

rule procedure can usually be devised for finding and selecting cases" (p. 141). To obtain a sample of pedestrians who frequent a downtown business district, for instance, interviewers can stand at street intersections on different days and at different times of day. Location, day, and time then become the criteria for the selection of individuals in this population. Additional criteria, such as selecting every *n*th person who enters a designated area or passes a certain point, could be included as well.

The researcher's primary task is to construct a sampling frame so that no cases in the population are systematically excluded. The quality of a sample depends on the avoidance of systematic bias in the selection of cases. For this reason, it will be some time before researchers can use e-mail addresses to send questionnaires to citizens. Virtually everyone in the target population will have to be linked to the "information superhighway" if such a method is to avoid the systematic exclusion of cases.

The best sampling designs employ *random selection,* a process for choosing cases from the sampling frame that permits all members of the population to have an equal (or at least known) chance of being selected, independent of any other event in the selection process. Random selection is the defining characteristic of a probability sample. The random selection of households or citizens (or whatever the unit of analysis is) is important because it eliminates any conscious or unconscious bias on the part of the researcher in choosing cases for the sample. In random selection, the characteristics of cases are unrelated to the selection process. Most important, random selection enables the researcher to employ probability theory, which is the basis for determining sampling error and confidence levels for samples of certain sizes. Probability sampling always requires the random selection of cases at some stage of the sampling process. Random selection is the hallmark of a scientific approach to survey research.

The Dangers of
Nonprobability Sampling

It is critical for public administrators to distinguish between probability samples and nonprobability samples. *Nonprobability sampling* methods have severe limitations, because they do not employ random selection of cases. In most instances, the money spent on surveys that use nonprobability sampling methods is wasted, because it is impossible to know how accurately the results of such surveys represent the larger population. A researcher cannot compute a confidence level or an error margin for a nonprobability sample.

The classic example of a nonprobability sample is a questionnaire published in a newspaper or magazine. Because not everyone in the target population reads or subscribes to the paper or magazine, this kind of survey violates a major principle of probability theory. In this case, population members have an unequal or unknown chance of being included in the survey.

Perhaps the most famous illustration of the disastrous use of nonprobability sampling occurred in connection with political polling in 1936. The *Literary Digest,* a popular newsmagazine of the time, sent 10 million postcard ballots to people listed in telephone directories and on lists of automobile owners across the United States. These citizens were asked to indicate who they would vote for in the next presidential election: the incumbent, Franklin Roosevelt, or the Republican contender, Alf Landon. More than 2 million people responded. This large N, or sampling fraction, bolstered the confidence of the survey's sponsors, who boldly predicted that Alf Landon would receive a stunning 57% of voters' support in the election, compared with a paltry 43% for Roosevelt.

In the actual election, held 2 weeks later, voters reelected Roosevelt to a second term in office with 61% of the vote, one of the largest popular landslides in history. The *Literary Digest*'s credibility was so greatly diminished that it was forced to cease publication shortly thereafter. What went wrong? How could such a large sample be so inaccurate? Quite simply, the poll used a biased sample. In the Depression year of 1936, less affluent Americans, those most likely to be Democrats and Roosevelt supporters, could not afford telephones and automobiles, and thus were systematically excluded from the sampling frame. The poll was biased in favor of more affluent Americans who could still afford phones and cars, who tended to be Republicans. The consequence of the biased sample selection in this case was a highly inaccurate estimate of the voting population's likely behavior. Clearly, how researchers go about selecting samples can greatly affect how accurately those samples can estimate the parameters of larger populations.

Asking for volunteers to participate in a survey is another example of nonprobability sampling. Volunteers are typically more interested in the topics of a survey than are citizens generally, so they are unlikely to be representative of the larger population. Moreover, volunteers are frequently different from the rest of the public in other ways. Many are likely to have higher incomes, more education, and more leisure time than other citizens. The use of only volunteer respondents injects a great deal of bias in any survey that aspires to measure the opinions of a large population.

A variation on the volunteer survey is the "person on the street" interview. If interviewers speak with passersby on one or two downtown street corners during one afternoon, it is highly unlikely that the results of such a survey will represent what all downtown shoppers think, for instance, about parking, shopping opportunities, personal safety, or whatever the study seeks to determine. Without a much more sophisticated sampling strategy that adequately covers different locations, times, and days of the week, the accuracy of any "quick pulse of the public" strategy is highly suspect and likely to be unrepresentative of the population of interest. Television news reporters are notorious for ignoring the unscientific nature of such exercises.

Still another example of a nonprobability sample, and a big waste of money, is the call-in radio or television survey. Typically, viewers or listeners are asked to call in their votes to different 900 telephone numbers to indicate if they agree or disagree on some topic or favor or oppose some decision. Because each call involves some charge, these surveys usually attract only those people who can afford the calls or who feel strongly enough (or bored enough) to spend some money to register their opinions. Such polls of self-selected volunteers are unlikely to yield results that represent the opinions of an entire population.

Another type of nonprobability sampling is quota sampling, which begins with a matrix that describes the characteristics of the target population that are important to the study and identifies the proportions that fall into the various categories, such as age, race, ethnicity, education, and income. Cases selected on the basis of these specified characteristics are supposed to reflect the distribution of the population's characteristics. For example, one might know what proportion of a state's population is white, is employed, is female, is over 40 years old, and has a college education. Each cell of the matrix is assigned a weight proportionate to its occurrence in the total population, and when all of the sample elements are so weighted, the results are supposed to represent the state's population profile. Screen questions are used to identify respondents with the desired attributes, according to the matrix, and then questions are asked of these individuals.

The most famous illustration of the dangers of using quota sampling is the Gallup Poll that predicted New York Governor Tom Dewey would defeat President Harry Truman in the 1948 presidential election. George Gallup selected his sample to ensure a "correct" proportion of respondents in each SES level and geographic area of the United States, based on the

1940 census. Even though Gallup's quota sample was based on the best data available, the distribution of the characteristics was not representative of the population. Massive demographic shifts from rural to urban areas had occurred after World War II. Urban residents, for example, were much more likely to vote Democratic. The underrepresentation of these voters and the overrepresentation of rural citizens resulted in highly inaccurate generalizations about how the entire population would vote. As everyone knows, Truman won the election by a slim margin of 4.4% (49.4% to 45.1%). The lesson of this case is that quota sampling should be avoided whenever accurate population data are unavailable.

The allure of inexpensive nonprobability samples is sometimes irresistible, but in most cases the bias inherent in sampling designs that lack random selection will produce inaccurate and misleading findings. The presence of sampling bias can be professionally fatal, especially when public opinion is almost evenly split on issues, programs, or even presidential candidates.

Probability Sampling Methods

There are several ways to select cases in a random manner for a sample. Five of the more commonly employed types of *probability sampling* are simple random sampling, systematic sampling, stratified sampling, cluster sampling, and multistage sampling. Most of the list-based methods are suitable for mail and personal interview survey projects. Simple random and stratified random sampling also can be incorporated into random digit dialing, which is a preferred method for developing a sampling pool for telephone surveys.

SIMPLE RANDOM SAMPLING

Simple random sampling is "simple" because there is only one step in the selection process once all the cases in the sampling frame are enumerated. In a simple random sample, every possible combination of cases has an equal chance of being selected. Selecting a simple random sample is a straightforward, if somewhat laborious, process that consists of three steps:

1. Obtain a complete list of the population.
2. Assign each case in the population a number.
3. Use a table of random numbers to select enough cases for the desired sample size.

Accurate lists are especially important for mail surveys. Researchers should check existing lists to be sure that annexed areas and new addresses are included. They should also "clean" lists to ensure that all of the addresses actually are located within the jurisdiction of interest. Ideally, the list should have the full names of current residents, so that the researcher can personalize cover letters, but this information is often not available; an accurate list of addresses alone is therefore acceptable. True random selection requires that every household, resident, or address have an equal chance of being selected. If the list is out-of-date or incomplete, the quality of the survey suffers.

Rarely are population lists perfectly accurate. Typically, directories and purchased lists of a city's housing units exclude people who reside in nursing homes, hospitals, college dormitories, motels, and military facilities. They also exclude people without addresses, such as migrant workers and the homeless. The researcher should explain any limitations or shortcomings of the sampling frame in the research report. A need to include some groups normally excluded from a population list may require site visits to various facilities or locales.

Simple random sampling is most often used for mail or personal interview surveys. Choosing a random sample for a telephone survey presents other challenges, which are discussed later in the section on random digit dialing. To illustrate selection of a simple random sample: assume that the researcher has a current list of the addresses of chief executive officers in the 2,829 local governments in the United States that have council-manager plans. The researcher assigns each manager (or case) a number, from 1 to 2,829, and then uses a table of random numbers (see Appendix A) to select the case numbers for a sample in an unbiased way. To use a random numbers table, one blindly places a pencil point somewhere on the table and begins the selection process at the place where the pencil lands. Because the population total in this hypothetical case (2,829) has four digits, the researcher looks at the first (or last) four digits of the number group where the pencil landed. The idea is to select the case with that number and then to move down a column or across a row to select subsequent four-digit groups until the desired sample size is obtained.

SYSTEMATIC SAMPLING

Systematic sampling is a variation of simple random sampling. It is an approximation of a truly random sample and is typically used with larger populations for which current population lists exist. Instead of numbering every case in the population, as in simple random sampling, the researcher determines the desired sample size and then calculates an interval that will run through the *entire* list to produce the desired sample size. Systematic selection requires the following steps:

1. Divide the number of cases in the population by the desired sample size to determine k. Let k equal the sampling interval.
2. Randomly select a case number in the random numbers table in the range 1 to k.
3. Proceed through the population list and select every kth case until the desired sample size is obtained.

To illustrate, suppose there are 20,000 households in a city and a sample of 400 is desired. The k interval equals 50 (20,000/400 = 50). Using a table of random numbers, the researcher blindly places a pencil point at a starting place and selects the first two numbers that are between 01 and 50. Assume the researcher finds the number 24; he or she begins the selection of cases with the 24th case on the list and then every 50th case thereafter (which is the 74th case, the 124th case, the 174th case, and so on) until 400 cases are selected from the list of 20,000 households. Technically, this procedure is called a systematic sample with a random start (Babbie, 1995).

One potential problem with this procedure is *periodicity.* Sometimes a population list is ordered in a nonrandom way that can bias the sample. For example, suppose a researcher wishes to survey participants in a housing subsidy program. If participants are listed by any defining factors, such as the amount of subsidy received, current income, or project of residence, an unrepresentative sample would be selected if the interval skips participants with particular characteristics. Such sampling frames should be randomized if possible.

Overall, systematic sampling is more convenient than simple random sampling because each case does not need to be assigned a unique case number. The researcher must be sure, however, that an ordered list does not systematically exclude the selection of cases.

STRATIFIED RANDOM SAMPLING

Stratified random sampling divides a population into two or more mutually exclusive strata for the purpose of selecting a random sample of each homogeneous stratum proportionate to its size in the population. When combined, these subsamples form a complete stratified sample of the population.

Stratified sampling can be a very efficient way to reduce sampling error and increase the representativeness of a sample. Recall the discussion earlier in this chapter that a researcher can reduce sampling error by increasing the sample size or by reducing population variability. Stratified sampling reduces population variability and lowers sampling error in estimating a population parameter by ensuring that different groups are adequately represented in the sample. In effect, it ensures that differences across the strata on some dependent variable of interest are accounted for and are not free to vary in the sample. A smaller stratified sample can provide the same level of precision as a larger simple random sample if the stratified variable is related to the dependent variable of interest.

To reduce sampling error, the researcher must select strata for division of the population that are related to the dependent variable of interest. Stratifying a population by classes unrelated to the dependent measure does not increase the precision of a sample estimate. The idea is to ensure that certain groups are adequately represented in the sample because the opinions of members of these groups differ across that stratum. Stratification systematically introduces a relevant source of opinion variability that might be missed if a group is underrepresented in the sample. The extent to which a sample accurately represents various attitudes, incomes, or ethnic groups may increase, for example, if the population of each geographic area of a jurisdiction is represented in proportion to its composition of the entire population.

Stratification is more efficient than simple random sampling when it accounts for differences across strata that otherwise might contribute to sampling error. Simple random samples can reduce sampling error only by increasing sample size. A researcher's ability to stratify the population depends, of course, on his or her having accurate information about the characteristics of population members. Obviously, if the time and cost to classify cases on various strata exceed the cost of selecting a larger simple random sample, then stratification is not a more efficient way to reduce sampling error. It also does not make much sense to use too many strata or subsamples, because the number of cases in a particular stratum could be too small for meaningful statistical analysis. One can imagine that classifying cases by criteria such as ideology, income, and race would quickly deplete the number of cases in the "conservative, high income, and black" cell. Rarely is it advantageous to stratify by more than two or three variables simultaneously (Blalock, 1979).

To illustrate the logic of stratified sampling, suppose a researcher wants to know what managers think about contracting out for park maintenance services. Previous research suggests that this practice may vary among regions. A simple random sample of 500 cases from a population of 2,683 cities might over- or underrepresent managers from a particular region. Stratifying the sample by region eliminates this source of variability. The researcher reduces sampling error by randomly selecting a proportionate number of managers from each region. When strata are sampled proportionate to their sizes in the population, each case still has an equal chance of being selected, but more precise estimates can be made about what managers in each region think of this practice.

Stratified sampling also can be used to guarantee that smaller groups in a population are represented in the sample proportionate to their size in the population. Conversely, if the study objectives require the researcher to make reliable and precise estimates about the opinions of various types of clients, then a *larger* number of clients within each group may be selected to satisfy a desired level of confidence and precision. This is called *disproportionate stratified sampling* and requires statistical weighting adjustments before generalizations about the population can be made. (These procedures are discussed later in this chapter.)

Either simple random or systematic selection methods can be used to choose cases for a stratum. For example, if the researcher knows the number of residential phone numbers in each prefix, such as 691 or 555, but an accurate and complete list of all numbers with this prefix is not available, the four-digit suffixes can be randomly selected (using a random numbers table) to obtain a proportionate sample of each prefix in a jurisdiction. If an accurate list of numbers in each prefix is available, the four-digit suffixes can be selected *systematically* to obtain a proportionate sample for each prefix.

Stratified random sampling appears to resemble quota sampling. Both methods divide the population into various strata, but the superficial resemblance ends there. In quota sampling, interviewers may arbitrarily select *anyone* they contact who meets the quota characteristics. Interviewers who are allowed to self-select respondents may introduce many different sources of bias, such as selecting only the "easy" or "cooperative" cases. By contrast, proportionate stratified sampling employs some form of *random sampling* to select cases in each stratum. In this case, the probability of case selection is known, but in quota sampling it is unknown.

CLUSTER SAMPLING

In cluster sampling, a population is divided into groups or clusters of interest. The purpose is to select a random sample of clusters. If *all* cases in *each* sample cluster are interviewed or sent questionnaires, this is *single-stage* cluster sampling, because sampling occurs only at the cluster selection stage. When a sample of cases from each randomly selected cluster is chosen, this is called *multistage* cluster sampling, because sampling occurs when the clusters are selected and when cases in each cluster are chosen.

Cluster sampling is useful when a list of the entire target population is unavailable or impractical to compile. This method can reduce the cost of data collection for large, dispersed populations. Clusters are usually geographic units, such as counties, cities, school districts, precincts, blocks, or census tracts. The cluster depends on the purpose of the survey. Unlike stratified sampling, which draws cases from *every* stratum in a population, cases are selected only from certain clusters.

To illustrate, suppose we want to obtain information from high school sophomores who enrolled in a state-mandated sex education and family planning course. A list of *all* students who took the course may not exist, and the cost and time to compile one would probably be prohibitive. Cluster sampling is a less costly alternative in this case. Using a list of all high schools in the state (the clusters), we might draw a *sample* of these and then contact the authorities at those high schools for lists of *all* students who completed the course during the year. A single-stage cluster sample requires that we interview or send questionnaires to all of the students on the lists of the selected high schools. In a multistage cluster sample design, a random sample of students on the rosters of the selected schools receive questionnaires. This strategy permits the researcher to sample more clusters, because fewer students in each are interviewed.

Cluster designs may employ simple or stratified random sampling at any stage. One might stratify clusters by size, type, or any attribute (stratum) that is important to the purpose of the study and that is related to the dependent measure being studied. Cluster sampling saves time and money because the researcher need not prepare a list of all cases in the population. Only the cases in the selected clusters need to be identified. In a single-stage design, all residents in the selected clusters are included in the sample; in a multistage cluster sample, only a random sample of members in the selected clusters are included in the study.

In single-stage cluster sampling, there is no sampling error *within* a cluster because everyone in the cluster is interviewed. Sampling error occurs only *between* clusters. Accordingly, it is important that the researcher select a sample of clusters proportionate to their size in the population. A stratification by geographic region also helps to ensure that the opinions of residents in any particular sector are represented. In multistage cluster sampling, it may be desirable to employ a stratified selection strategy to ensure that certain groups are represented in the sample proportionate to their size of the entire population. The accuracy of population information and the method of contact governs the feasibility of this strategy. If data are out-of-date, it is impossible to compute accurate proportions. Screen questions in telephone interviews help researchers to control who in a given household responds, but mail questionnaires do not offer the same assurance, despite cover letter requests that only certain types of individuals complete the instruments.

How many clusters should be selected in a single-stage design? How many cases should be chosen in each cluster in a multistage design? The objective is to minimize sampling error. As noted, single-stage designs minimize error *within* a cluster (because everyone is included in the sample). However, sampling error still exists when the sample of clusters is selected. Sampling error is present at each stage of a multistage design. For these reasons, cluster samples can be more cost-efficient, but they also may compound sampling error and result in less precise estimates of population parameters, size for size, than either simple random or stratified samples.

It is best to sample as many clusters as resources permit, and to reduce the number of elements or cases sampled in each (Babbie, 1995). Clearly, there is an inherent trade-off between increasing the representativeness of clusters at the risk of more poorly representing the population within each cluster. However, if the clusters are relatively small geographic units, such as census blocks, the cases making up each cluster are likely to be relatively *homogeneous*. Consequently, fewer cases are needed to represent a natural cluster adequately, even though a larger number of clusters are required to represent sufficiently the diversity among the clusters (Babbie, 1995). If the number of clusters is increased, "sampling error will be reduced at the stage that is subject to the greatest error" (Singleton et al., 1993, p. 157).

Whenever clusters differ in size, as they most likely will, Babbie (1995) advises the use of a modified cluster sampling design called *probability proportionate to size,* or PPS (p. 217). The purpose of this strategy is to ensure that clusters with different numbers of households have a probability of being selected proportionate to their size. For example, blocks with densely populated apartment buildings may have 300 households, whereas more sparsely populated blocks of single-family units may have only 100 households. Following the logic of PPS, a city block with 300 households should have three times the chance of being selected as one with only 100

TABLE 3.3 Selecting Blocks With a Probability Proportionate to Size

Cambridge City Block	Number of Households	Cumulative Number of Households
1	120	120
2	37	157
3	41	198
4	76	274
.	.	.
.	.	.
.	.	.
100	19	2,500

households. Within each block the same number of interviews are conducted, but the PPS method ensures that residents of a few large clusters are not excluded altogether, as they *could* be if clusters were chosen by simple random selection.

Before a sample of blocks can be selected proportionate to the number of households in each, the researcher must first decide how large a sample is needed to satisfy confidence and accuracy criteria. Assume, for example, that the city of Cambridge has 2,500 households and 100 blocks. The researcher can afford a sample of 500 households from 25 blocks, so 20 households in each block will be interviewed. The city blocks differ in size. The researcher lists the total number of households in each of the 100 blocks, as illustrated in Table 3.3.

The households in Block 1 are assigned numbers 1 through 120. Block 2 is assigned numbers 121 through 157, Block 3 is assigned 158 through 198, and so forth until each block is allocated its proportion of households in the city. To select 25 blocks in a way that ensures a chance of selection proportionate to the number of households in each, it is necessary to calculate a sampling interval following the same procedure used for a systematic random sample. In this example, the sampling interval is 100 (2,500/25). A random start is selected between 1 and 100. Assume that, using a table of random numbers, the researcher blindly inserts a pencil point that lands on 052. Because 52 is within the range of numbers assigned to Block 1, it is selected. Adding 100 to 52 means that Block 2 will be selected, because 152 is within the 121-157 range for that block. Adding 100 and 152 means that Block 4 will be selected, because 252 is within the range of numbers assigned to that block. This procedure is continued until 25 blocks are selected.

A block with 120 households is about three times more likely to be selected with this method than a block with only 41 households. This procedure also ensures that the *overall* probability of *any* household being selected is the *same,* regardless of the block size. For example, if the city has 100 blocks and 2,500 households, and we want to select a total of 500 households for a sample, each household should have a 500/2,500, or .2, chance of selection.

A block has a probability of selection equal to the number of blocks to be chosen times the number of households in the block, divided by the number of households in the entire city, as in the following:

25 blocks to be chosen × (Block 1's 120 households)/(2,500 households in the city) = 1.2 .

If Block 1 is selected, each household has a second-stage probability of being selected equal to the number of households selected on each block divided by the number of households on that block:

(20 households selected)/(120 households on block) = .167 .

The overall probability of selecting a household on that block is obtained by multiplying 1.2 by .167, which equals .2. This example demonstrates that a block's chances of being selected depend on its size, but each household's overall chances of selection are the same, regardless of the block. Because the probability of selection for each case is known, cluster sampling satisfies the criterion for being a probability sample.

Table 3.4 summarizes the major advantages and disadvantages of each of the five types of sampling designs.

Weighting Cases

Disproportionate sampling and *weighting* of cases are methods that researchers occasionally use, resources permitting, to study groups in a population when a simple random or systematic sample of the entire population would include too few members of those groups for meaningful analysis. Suppose, for example, that anecdotal evidence suggests that black and Hispanic central-city residents hold different opinions about the effectiveness of a police bicycle patrol program. If Hispanics and blacks constitute 25% and 15% of all downtown households, respectively, a simple random

TABLE 3.4 The Merits of Probability Sampling Strategies

Sampling Strategy	Advantages	Disadvantages
Simple random sampling	Accuracy and sampling error are easily estimated; requires minimum advance knowledge of population characteristics.	Complete population list required; can be expensive, especially for personal or face-to-face interviews.
Systematic sampling	Convenient and quick method of obtaining a sample from a large list of the population.	Periodicity is a potential problem; requires a list of the entire population; expensive for personal interviews.
Stratified random samples	Ensures representation of various groups in the population.	Requires accurate information on the proportion of the population in each stratum.
Cluster sampling	Lower costs if the clusters are geographically defined.	Somewhat less accurate than other methods.
Multistage cluster sampling	Lower costs than simple random samples for larger populations; less error than single-stage cluster sampling.	Subject to greater error than simple random sampling; can be more expensive than cluster sampling.

SOURCES: Hessler (1992) and Weisberg, Krosnick, and Bowen (1989).

or systematic sample of the entire population should have about these same proportions of Hispanics and blacks. A random sample of 500 downtown households (selected from a total of 2,500 households, for instance) has an error margin of 4% at the 95% confidence level for opinion estimates. However, this sample will have only about 125 Hispanics and 75 blacks in it. Obviously, the opinion estimates for members of just these two groups, with this number represented in the sample, will not be very accurate.

To increase the accuracy of opinion estimates for specific population groups, the investigator may employ disproportionate sampling to select enough members of each group to satisfy the desired criteria of a 4% error margin at the 95% confidence level. From Table 3.1, we surmise that a sample of about 313 Hispanics and another sample of 189 blacks will have a 4% error margin. A third sample of all other downtown households (the remaining 1,500) requires about 441 cases to satisfy these criteria. The results from the three samples are analyzed separately. Comparisons of each group's opinions (at the same level of accuracy and confidence) are now possible.

As long as the samples are analyzed separately, weighting of cases is irrelevant. If the researcher wants to make generalizations about the opinions of *all* downtown residents as a group, the three subsamples need to be weighted and then combined to create a composite profile of downtown residents' opinions. The results of each subsample are weighted by the proportion of the total population that the stratum constitutes. For example, the average Hispanic approval rating for the bicycle patrol program is multiplied by .25, the average approval rating for blacks is multiplied by .15, and the remaining households' mean approval rating is multiplied by .60. These values are summed to obtain an estimate of the mean approval rating for the entire population. Software programs such as SPSS facilitate this task by employing a weight command that assigns precise weights to all cases.

Obtaining Samples for Telephone Surveys

There are two major categories of sampling designs for telephone surveys: those that depend upon lists, such as telephone or reverse directories, and those that utilize some version of random digit dialing (RDD). RDD techniques often start with the working telephone prefixes in the jurisdiction of interest and then employ random selection of number suffixes to create a sample stratified by prefix. (An excellent source of additional information on sampling methodologies for telephone surveys is the work of Groves et al., 1988.)

Lists are important for mail and personal interview surveys, but they are not the preferred sources for telephone survey sampling frames. Among the problems with phone directories are unlisted numbers. In Las Vegas and in the Los Angeles-Long Beach area, for instance, more than 60% of telephone numbers are unlisted. Smaller jurisdictions have unlisted rates as low as 20%, but even within a particular state, cities vary in rates of unlisted numbers. In Tennessee, for example, Knoxville has an unlisted rate of 24.5%, Memphis has a 26.9% rate, and Nashville has a 30.6% rate. If new but unpublished listings are added to these figures, we can see that perhaps as many as a third or more of telephone subscribers are omitted from telephone directories.

The crux of the problem is that persons with unlisted numbers may differ on a number of characteristics from those with published phone numbers. Those with unlisted numbers tend to be younger, have lower incomes, live in urban areas, fear crime more, and move frequently, and tend to be unmarried women and nonwhite (Frey, 1989). Consequently, a sample of numbers from a telephone directory can be biased. The systematic exclusion of any group or segment of a population violates the basic principle of probability sampling, that every member of the population have an equal or known chance of being selected.

A second shortcoming of phone directory lists is that they are usually out-of-date by the time they are published. The time lag between data collection and publication is often several months, and their accuracy diminishes with time. Also, in about 1% of all listings, wrong numbers are printed in directories. Nonetheless, directories may be an acceptable basis for selecting a sample for some smaller cities that have slow or no growth and experience little change between annual publications.

If the operators of the 911 emergency service in a jurisdiction are cooperative, researchers may be able to obtain an accurate printout or computer disk with all of the numbers connected to this service. This can be one of the most current lists of active phone numbers available.

About 95 to 97% of the households in the United States have phones. The proportion of households in a population that have telephone service is called the *penetration rate*. The telephone penetration rate varies by state and by region within states. The risk of systematically missing some people when interviewing by telephone exists, but most researchers do not consider this to be such a serious problem that they reject the distinct advantages of telephone surveys (Frey, 1989).

RANDOM DIGIT DIALING

Random digit dialing is a common method for obtaining a sample for a phone survey. This technique overcomes the problems of inaccurate and outdated directory listings, and, theoretically, each household with a phone has an equal chance of being called regardless of whether the number is listed.

The telephone numbers used to complete a predetermined number of interviews constitute the *sampling pool.* To generate a sampling pool, the researcher must identify the working three-digit prefixes that ring in the geographic boundaries of the target population. It is useful for the researcher to ascertain the approximate number of telephone access lines in operation for each prefix, and then use this information to generate random telephone numbers in proportion to the number of lines in that prefix. In this way, the sample is stratified by prefix. In smaller cities, for example, only one prefix may be in use, so there is no need to stratify the sample. However, it may be necessary to screen residents with the same prefix who live outside the city.

Information about vacuous banks of suffixes (numerical ranges of telephone numbers that are inoperative or contain no residential lines) is also useful. Usually, the local telephone company can provide these data. In larger cities, this information often is published in reverse directories, which are ordered by telephone numbers rather than names.

RDD samples also can be generated manually or by computer, or can be purchased from commercial vendors in the sampling business. This last method is probably the most widely used by survey consultants, because it is the easiest way to obtain a random sample of working telephone numbers. Companies produce sample lists of phone numbers proportionate to the numbers of lines in each of the working prefixes in the jurisdiction. They also determine that the first number of each suffix is among the working banks or blocks of phone numbers in the jurisdiction. They then randomly generate the remaining three numbers of each suffix. In effect, the sheets of numbers they provide contain a representative sample of numbers in a working prefix and suffix block. In addition, the sheets they prepare often include columns that interviewers can use for recording the disposition of the contacts they make. A sample of 1,800 numbers produced by such companies, for example, costs about $500. For organizations that regularly conduct telephone surveys, it may be cost-effective to purchase all phone numbers in the United States in CD-ROM format.

In generating a random list of telephone numbers manually, a random numbers table is used. For example, if a city has only two prefixes, 458 and 459, the investigator randomly selects a starting place on the random numbers table to create a sampling pool. The random sequence of numbers in a random numbers table might be 1009732533765201. If both the 458 and the 459 have about the same proportion of the total number of phone lines in the city, the first four numbers in the sample will be 458-1009, 459-7325, 458-3376, and 459-5201. The formerly well-sighted person who creates the sample pool continues this tedious process until a sufficient sample size is generated.

If the proportion of numbers in a 458 prefix is 40%, for example, and the 459 prefix reaches 60% of the households, then the person generating the sampling pool adds strings of four digits to the prefixes chosen in the following order: 458, 458, 458, 458, 459, 459, 459, 459, 459, 459. This distribution reflects the relative proportion of the prefixes in the jurisdiction. Computer routines for generating random numbers make this task easier.

Estimating the Size of
the Sampling Pool for Telephone Surveys

The size of the sampling pool of telephone numbers can be estimated using a formula developed by Lavrakas (1987):

$$\text{Size of Sampling Pool} = \frac{(FSS)}{(HR)\,(1-REC)\,(1-LE)},$$

where FSS = the *final sample size,* or the number of completed interviews needed to obtain the confidence and accuracy level desired; HR = the *hit rate,* or the estimate of the proportion of telephone numbers in the sampling pool that are likely to ring at the appropriate locations (e.g., residences); REC = *respondent exclusion criteria,* or the factors that would lead to respondents' being ruled ineligible; and LE = the *loss of eligibles,* or the refusal rate among the individuals in the sampling pool.

Even the most current sample of telephone numbers contains some non-working numbers and perhaps some nonresidential numbers. The proportion of such numbers will vary by jurisdiction and the method used to generate the list of numbers. If information is available about working numbers for each prefix and banks of vacuous suffixes, fewer nonworking numbers will be called. Even lists purchased from polling companies may contain some nonworking or business numbers. For this reason, it is prudent to estimate a hit rate between 40% and 50% (.40 or .50 for the formula).

The need to screen any persons or households who are ineligible to participate in the survey increases the required sample size. A question such as "Do you reside within the corporate limits of the city of Austin?" screens citizens who may live in Travis County but outside the Austin city limits and have the same telephone prefix as city residents. If the target population consists only of city residents and some prefixes cover territory outside the corporate limits, the researcher should estimate the number of these lines to ensure that the sample is large enough to attain the desired number of responses from city residents after nonresidents are rejected. Usually, the local telephone company can provide such estimates. Some phone companies also prepare maps of the areas covered by various prefixes. With such maps and district-level census data, the researcher can estimate the number of households located outside the city with the same prefix as city residents.

The REC might also involve other screen questions. For instance, if female-headed households constitute the target population and the census indicates that this group makes up 25% of all households, then typically three of every four households contacted will not have such a person living there. In this case, the REC value would be .75 (i.e., $1 - .25$). This type of telephone survey is expensive. Fortunately, most opinion surveys direct calls to persons 18 years or older and assume a small REC value, because most households include someone who is at least 18.

Even when very experienced and talented interviewers are employed, the LE value may range from .15 to .25, which means that 15 to 25% of the persons contacted refuse to participate in the survey. Techniques for minimizing the loss of eligibles are discussed in Chapter 4.

Computing the sample size for a telephone survey is a straightforward task. Suppose the target population is 25,000, and we want to be 95% sure that the margin of error is no greater than ± 4%. Consulting the sample size table, we find that the FSS, or final size of the sample, should be 610. We estimate the hit rate to be 40%. The REC value is determined to be .05 because we are interested in interviewing residents 18 years or older, and at least 95% of all households in the hypothetical target population are headed by someone who is at least this age. A best guess at the LE is .30, because this is a relatively small city whose citizens have a mean educational attainment higher than the state average, and thus are likely to be somewhat more cooperative.

Using the formula, we calculate:

$$\text{Size of Sample Pool} = \frac{610}{(.40)\,(1 - .05)\,(1 - .30)} = 2{,}293 \,.$$

On the basis of my experience, I believe it is prudent to add about 5% to 10% more cases to the number derived from the formula to ensure that the sampling pool is large enough. Consequently, about 2,500 numbers should be purchased for the city in this example. Not all of these numbers will be processed; the purpose is to ensure that a sufficient quantity is on hand to complete 610 interviews. Interviewers should call each number three or four times to try to reach residents. A larger sampling pool guarantees that it will not be depleted in the event of a large number of unsuccessful callbacks, nonworking numbers, ineligible respondents, and refusals.

Screening Respondents
for Telephone Interviews

The goal in processing the sampling pool is to obtain representative estimates of the target population's parameters. The target population may consist of households, adult citizens, or members of a particular clientele group. If the unit of analysis is the household, *any* adult in the household may respond to the questions. Generalizations are then appropriate about what all households think. If the purpose of the survey is to estimate what all adults over 18 think, the investigator needs to employ selection procedures to ensure that the individuals who answer the survey questions are selected in proportion to their numbers in the population.

When telephone numbers are sampled, it is really the phone lines connected to those addresses that are being sampled. Screening procedures convert a sample of household telephone lines into a sample of *all* adult residents in a jurisdiction. In this case, a probability sample is possible only when "the selection of the respondent is not at the discretion of the interviewer or where the most convenient respondent is not always chosen" (Frey, 1989, pp. 104-105).

Without a screening procedure, the researcher obtains a sample that consists only of the individuals who typically answer the phones in their households. Experience has proven that these are most likely to be females. Without screening, then, women tend to be overrepresented in telephone samples, whereas men are underrepresented. Consequently, investigators need to employ selection procedures that will ensure that population members are selected in proportion to their numbers in the entire population.

Several screening strategies give any adult in the randomly selected household a chance to be selected, and Frey (1989) and Lavrakas (1987) review the merits of some of these options. One technique that I find particularly easy to use and that is among the least obtrusive is the "birthday method." Asking the person who answers the phone about who in the household had the last birthday or who will have the next birthday is an unobtrusive and nonthreatening probability technique. It is based on the premise that every adult member of a household has an equal chance of being chosen because of the random nature of the selection. This method does not require individuals to reveal their ages; they need only tell who in the household had the most recent birthday or will have the next one.

For example, after delivering some introductory remarks (the *introductory spiel*) that indicate his or her identity and the purpose and importance of the survey, the interviewer asks:

> We need to be sure that we give every adult in [name of the jurisdiction] a chance to be interviewed for this study. Among those 18 years or older in your household, I need to speak to the person who had the most recent [or who has the next] birthday. Are you that individual?

If the answer is yes, the interviewer continues with the questions. If it is no, the interviewer asks to speak with the appropriate person. If the eligible respondent is not available, the interviewer asks for that person's first name and inquires about the best time to call back to speak with him or her.

In practice, the "last birthday" method is preferable to the "next birthday" alternative, because it is usually easier for individuals to recall the past than to construct the future (Frey, 1989). The birthday method enables the researcher to translate a sample of households into a sample of adults because a nonbiased selection procedure ensures that every adult has an equal chance of selection. If midway through the sampling pool a particular group is still underrepresented (compared with accurate census profile data), interviewers can be instructed to make specific requests to speak with members of that underrepresented group (the youngest male in the household, for instance).

Timely data entry for completed interviews or use of computer-assisted telephone interview programs allows the survey supervisor to track progress in obtaining a representative sample of the population on the attributes considered important for the purposes of the study. The distinct advantage of random selection is that even if recent census data are not available for comparison, the researcher can rely on probability theory to calculate the confidence in the accuracy of the sample's estimates.

Processing Sampling Pools

It is important to establish a policy for releasing phone numbers from the sampling pool. The survey supervisor has the primary responsibility for consistent policy implementation. Phone numbers, listed on call sheets (see Appendix B), should be released to each caller a page or two at a time. The supervisor should check the disposition of the calls made by each interviewer. At least three callbacks, preferably four, should be made to numbers that do not answer. No more than two of these callbacks should be made on the same afternoon or evening.

The goal for the supervisor is to release the *minimum* number of telephone numbers from the sampling pool necessary to obtain the desired sample size. This practice helps to ensure that a diligent effort is made to contact residents who are difficult to reach. The supervisor should strive to keep the number of calls in an unresolved condition (rings but no answer) to a minimum by scheduling callbacks for different times.

The supervisor needs to make sure that all callers understand how to record the disposition of each dialing. The date and time of each call and a disposition code should be recorded on the call sheet. Typical outcomes include ring/no answer, busy, out of order, refusal, completed, answering machine, business or government office, answered by nonresident (such as a baby-sitter), and noneligible.

The growing prevalence of telephone answering machines has made it more difficult to reach individuals by telephone than was the case in the past. Many people use these machines to screen all their calls, which means interviewers need to be trained to handle such cases. Essentially, the recommended practice is to leave a polite message that identifies the caller, the organization represented, and the purpose of the call. A promise to call back at another time when the individual is able to come to the phone lets the potential respondent know that additional attempts will be made to obtain his or her opinions and ideas that are "so essential for obtaining accurate information about what people think about the county's services and programs." If the caller is polite and sincere, a resident who is really at home may be more likely to pick up the receiver and give the caller a chance to persuade the individual to participate in the survey.

Calculating Response Rates

Samples have known sampling errors if the procedures described in this chapter are followed. However, other sources of error may bias the survey results. *Measurement errors* occur when questions are worded imprecisely (Nachmias & Nachmias, 1992). Another particularly worrisome source of error is *nonsampling error,* which may stem from a large number of non-responses or careless data entry. The sample sizes for different confidence levels and error margins in Tables 3.1 and 3.2 are predicated on a 100% completion rate. When individuals in a sample refuse, hang up, or fail to return questionnaires, these nonresponses may bias the survey findings and diminish the survey's quality. The higher the response rate, the more precise are the sample's estimates of the population parameters, assuming that no group is systematically underrepresented. If one or more groups are underrepresented due to nonresponses, the results may not accurately represent the population.

The formula for computing the response rate for a survey is as follows:

$$\text{Response Rate} = 1 - [(n - r)/n] \,,$$

where n = the sample size and r = the number of responses obtained. For example, if 240 mail questionnaires are received from a sample of 600 residents, the response rate is $1 - [(600 - 240)/600] = .40$, or 40%. If the population is 15,000 and we want to be 95% sure that the estimates are 4% of the population parameters, a sample size of 240 would fall short of the desired level of precision. If no group is systematically underrepresented among the 240 responses, the *best* we can claim is that the results are about ±7% of a population parameter.

The energy devoted to the details of survey design helps to eliminate the instrument defects that may cause a potential respondent to hang up the phone or fail to return a questionnaire. The best randomly selected sample cannot deliver the desired level of accuracy unless the required number of responses is obtained. Getting that maximum response rate is the researcher's reward for investing time in a carefully planned and well-designed survey instrument.

An apparent advantage of telephone interviews is that the desired number of completed interviews can always be obtained. Investigators must be extremely careful, however, not to obtain the desired sample size at the cost of drawing an unrepresentative sample of easy-to-reach people. Quickly replacing phone numbers without first making diligent efforts to reach the persons connected to them results in a sample of easy-to-reach people. These individuals may be different from, and may hold different views from, others who are not so easily reached. A biased sample negates all of the efforts made to employ random selection. For this reason, the telephone survey supervisor should be conservative about releasing numbers from the sampling pool. This same logic explains why follow-up mailings and visits are made in mail and personal interview projects.

Summary

Sampling is the process of selecting cases from a population; in survey research, it is imperative that samples be selected in unbiased ways. Probability theory permits the researcher to have a certain level of confidence in the accuracy of a sample's estimates as long as random selection is incorporated in the sampling design at some stage. The confidence in and accuracy of any sample's estimates are primarily functions of sample size and population variability. The size of a sample is a function of the desired level of confidence and precision in the sample statistics, the population's variability, the type of analyses needed for subgroups of the population, and the project's budget. The primary types of probability sampling designs are simple random sampling, systematic sampling, stratified random sampling, and cluster sampling. Probability samples are distinguished from nonprobability samples by random selection and by the fact that in a probability sample each case has an equal or at least known probability of being selected.

So far, this and preceding chapters have addressed the researcher's need to specify the purposes and objectives of the survey, decisions to be made concerning the target population and appropriate unit of analysis, the choices among methods of contact, and selection of a probability sample of the desired size. The next stage in the survey research process is the design of the actual instrument, which is the subject of Chapter 4.

4

Survey Design
and Implementation

Creating questions that elicit accurate responses from the persons in the sample requires an appreciation of both the art and the science of questionnaire design. A key assumption that underlies this effort is that people generally want to tell the truth. Survey research is predicated on the idea that lying is not a source of systematic bias. Researchers must craft response choices that make it easy for respondents to be truthful, honest, and candid.

Artistically, survey design requires a keen sense of page layout, vertical question flow, and logical question sequence, features that invite rather than deter participation. Clear, cogent questions with interesting and appropriate response choices prompt accurate, consistent responses. Moreover, the questions should interest respondents. The instrument should be easy to follow and to interpret, both for the interviewer and for the respondents. Visual appeal is especially important for mail surveys, but clear instructions and cogent questions are important regardless of the method of contact. Clarity, simplicity, and attractiveness are the hallmarks of a professional, polished product. The dividend is a high response rate.

The science of asking questions essentially concerns whether an item is a valid measure of what the researcher wants to know about the respondents. Do the questions mean the same thing to all respondents? A great response rate to a survey with poorly worded questions is pregnant with error and only misinforms and misleads. The challenge for the researcher is to write questions that are valid and reliable measures of what he or she wants to know and to avoid things that diminish these qualities. The most serious of these are ambiguity and bias in how questions are worded, ordered, or asked.

Writing questions to measure concepts is much less exact than the statistical methods available for analyzing the results. The researcher should always be mindful that the use of sophisticated sampling and statistical techniques does not, by itself, ensure that the results will be useful or meaningful for the policy process. What matters is how questions and response choices are worded and whether these measure what the researcher intends. In *The Art of Asking Questions,* Payne (1951) recognizes the laborious but critical nature of this task. His advice is deceptively simple but still appropriate, because question wording remains the most serious defect of contemporary surveys: "We need to develop a critical attitude toward our questions . . . [and] subordinate any pride of authorship to this critical attitude" (p. 16). "As question worders, we must be sure that our meaning is comprehended by others" (p. 21).

Previous researchers have devised measures for many political and psychological concepts in social science. It is always wise for researchers designing surveys to review the survey questions developed by others on topics similar to their projects and to contact the authors of relevant surveys for copies of their instruments. Survey questions are often published in journals such as *Public Opinion Quarterly.* Indexes are published for surveys conducted by the *New York Times*/CBS, Gallup, and the National Opinion Research Center's General Social Surveys. The U.S. Census is also an excellent source for attribute questions related to employment, occupation, family, race, ethnicity, income, wealth, education, marital status, household status, and housing types.

The researcher's literature review on a survey topic should begin with articles that have appeared in public administration journals. *Public Administration Review, American Review of Public Administration,* and *Social Science Quarterly,* as well as specialized public policy journals, are good sources of ideas. The researcher should not assume, however, that

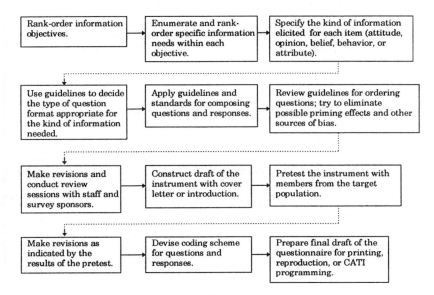

Figure 4.1. An Overview of the Survey Design Process

publication in a scholarly journal means that a question has attained a permanent state of grace with respect to either its validity or its reliability. *All* questions adapted or created for a new survey instrument must be pretested. Language evolves, and the meaning and importance of questions are affected by the context and even their location in the questionnaire (Converse & Presser, 1986). A response that something is "cool," for example, has a positive connotation for some people. Similarly, at one time "government investment" and "contributions" were not perceived as political codes for higher spending and taxes.

The use of unambiguous words is necessary but not sufficient to avoid bias. The location of a question in the instrument affects the reliability and validity of answers to it. For instance, a well-phrased question about school performance placed *after* a series of questions about a teacher walkout or strike will yield an entirely different response distribution from the one it would elicit if it were placed before this series.

There is much to consider in this stage of the survey research process, as Figure 4.1 illustrates. The ultimate utility of a survey depends on how well the researcher applies the guidelines that constitute the art and science of questionnaire design and wording. If a single maxim could summarize this stage of the process, it is as follows: *Know what you want to ask and why you want to ask it; compose clear, unambiguous questions, keep the survey as brief as possible, and have a plan for analyzing the results before the instrument is administered.*

The Basics of Question Order

Which structure or format is best for a question? What kind of response choices should be offered? Which type of question is best for the kind of information needed? How much should the question format vary so the respondent does not become bored? Before tackling each of these important issues, the researcher will find it prudent to think first about the general order of items in the instrument. One way to proceed from the proverbial blank sheet of paper to the first rough draft for peer review is to follow these suggestions:

1. Specify and rank-order, from most to least important, the information objectives of the survey.
2. Enumerate the kinds of information needed from respondents that relate to each information objective. Are they opinions, attitudes, beliefs, or attributes? Group related items, such as opinions about the effectiveness of a service or program.
3. Rank the items *within* each topical group in the order of their importance to the study.
4. For *each* item in *each* group, try to answer these questions:

   Why ask this? (How is it linked to the central purpose of the survey?)

   Who in the target population knows about it, and are they likely to have an opinion about it?

   How will the responses to this item be coded?

   What kind of statistical analysis will be performed with this variable? (What limits attend the variable's likely level of measurement?)
5. Place the *most* interesting item(s) in the *most* important battery of questions at the beginning of the questionnaire.

The preferred strategy is to begin the questionnaire with the most interesting and most important questions. The objective is to grab the respondent's attention, to pique interest. The initial questions should correspond very closely to the stated purpose of the study. The last section of the instrument normally contains the attribute questions. In between, the instrument should include nothing that will confuse or embarrass the respondent.

These suggestions produce a logical outline of the order of items that reflects the central objectives of the research. Now the researcher needs to tackle some more discrete questions, such as those posed in the first paragraph of this section. Decisions about question type and format involve a basic choice between open-ended and some type of closed-ended questions. This choice is governed by the level of information about the topic possessed by the respondent *and* the researcher, the *type* of information needed, and the types of analyses the researcher wants to perform with the data.

Question Types

The two basic question types are open-ended and closed-ended. Respondents answer open-ended questions in their own words. For closed-ended questions, the researcher offers limited response choices. The researcher must review the advantages and disadvantages of each in the context of the decision about how best to structure a particular question.

OPEN-ENDED QUESTIONS

Open-ended questions are appropriate under the following circumstances:

- When the researcher has difficulty devising a reasonable number of mutually exclusive categories for a response set
- When it is reasonable to expect that the respondent has some information about or keen interest in the topic
- When it is important for the purposes of the study that respondents feel free to state, in their own words, what they think or how they feel about a particular topic, issue, or proposal
- When decision makers need to probe what people think or feel, even though no one has complete information about a particular problem, issue, or proposal
- When the item solicits nominal data, but including a list of possible answers would be too long for a mail questionnaire or too time-consuming and difficult to communicate orally
- When the researcher needs to measure especially sensitive or socially undesirable behaviors, in which case more people will respond to open-ended questions than to closed-ended questions (Sudman & Bradburn, 1982)

Under these circumstances, the *judicious* and *sparing* use of open-ended questions can stimulate the interest of respondents, generate information that no other question type can ascertain, and offer insights about issues that preconceived response choices may overlook.

Open-ended questions offer the researcher an opportunity to identify specific problems or circumstances known only to specific groups of respondents. Subdivision residents, for example, may know about the location of drainage or flooding problems. A closed-ended question about the seriousness of flooding problems in their neighborhood can be followed by an open-ended question about where these are located.

Open-ended questions are particularly well suited for *exploratory* research questions as long as respondents have some knowledge or information about the topic. The topic likewise should engage the attention and interest of the respondent. Open-ended questions, for example, can be used to ascertain respondents' knowledge about whether a local lake is safe for swimming. The results may suggest revisions in a public safety information campaign. Open-ended questions are futile if the respondents do not have *any* knowledge of or interest in a topic. Increasing the police budget may be a keen concern for the police chief, but most citizens cannot make informed judgments about whether or how much such a budget should be increased.

Open-ended questions are very demanding for respondents. They require more time, effort, and skill to complete than do closed-ended questions. Accordingly, they should be used sparingly. On the instrument for a self-administered survey, the survey designer should allow enough space for a four- or five-line response, but no lines should be inserted in the instrument, as this can constrain comments. Telephone or personal interviews receive more responses to open-ended questions when the target population has a high proportion of illiterates or persons with low educational attainment. These contact methods also permit interviewers to ask follow-up and probe questions to clarify responses.

Open-ended questions are more difficult to code than are closed-ended questions. For mail questionnaires, the researcher can read all of the responses to open-ended questions and then develop categories and codes for various answers. For telephone or personal interview projects, interviewers must record accurately the essence of the respondents' comments, and then categories and codes are devised by one or two people who make judgments about category assignments. This procedure helps to ensure consistency, and later peer review of this effort can help to ascertain the reasonableness and reliability of these decisions.

CLOSED-ENDED QUESTIONS

Closed-ended questions are accompanied by lists of possible answers from which respondents choose. Response choice lists that have no "other," "no opinion," or "don't know/not sure" options are called *forced-choice* formats. Good closed-ended questions are difficult to develop, but they have several distinct advantages:

- They are easier for respondents to answer, provided the respondents are familiar with the subject and have thought enough about it to take a position or to form an opinion.
- A good response list offers a common frame of reference to maximize reliability.
- The responses are easily coded, which facilitates comparisons within or across different groups in the target population.
- Attribute and behavior questions are especially well suited to a closed-ended format because the choices can be expressed as ranges.
- Ordered response choices permit the researcher to classify individuals, measure the intensity of attitudes, and perform ordinal-level data analyses.

It can be difficult to craft closed-ended questions for several reasons. The researcher has to decide how much information members of the population have about a topic and whether they are likely to have an opinion about it. The problem of nonattitudes is very real (as discussed in Chapter 2); questions must be directed to and answered by people who are likely to know something about the subject.

The choices that make up the response set must be ones that people commonly understand and will interpret reliably. O'Sullivan and Rassel (1995) report that they once asked respondents to indicate the ethnicity of volunteers, but "only after we received several surveys indicating that 'all' volunteers were Native Americans did we realize that our terminology was interpreted differently by our respondents" (p. 192). There is always the risk that someone will misinterpret the meaning of a question or a particular response choice. The objective is to make the question and the options as plainly intelligible as possible. Plain language, common concepts, and clear task explanations facilitate comprehension. Careful pretesting of closed-ended questions increases the likelihood that they will be common-ly understood.

A clear response set can salvage an unclear or poorly worded question. A student of mine once submitted an attribute question that read, "Please indicate the number in your household broken down by sex." I wanted to answer "zero," because we are still in good shape, but explicit choices concerning numbers of males and females precluded this response. Response categories can be important cues for understanding questions.

Good closed-ended questions satisfy two measurement principles: *exhaustiveness* and *mutual exclusiveness.* Exhaustive response categories include *all* of the possible responses that might be expected. If they are inadequate, respondents may not be able to indicate their genuine opinions. An incomplete response set suggests that answers are limited to the listed options. Rational people will either skip questions that have incomplete response choices or mark something that *seems* close to their view. Nonexhaustive categories result in an instrument robust in error and low in response, because people quickly conclude that the entire enterprise is a waste of time if none of the choices applies to them.

Mutually exclusive responses offer clear, distinct, and nonoverlapping choices. Instructions to choose the "one best answer" from a list can help to eliminate confusion. Researchers should always avoid overlapping response choices, such as $10,000-$20,000 and $20,000-$30,000. Similarly, researchers should never list choices that are very close in meaning. The use of *frequently, sometimes, occasionally,* and *regularly* in the same response set is confusing. Other words to avoid using in the same response set are *usually, seldom, often,* and *rarely.* The principle is that one should avoid vague terms that are subject to different interpretations by reasonable people. Subtle differences among choices jeopardize the validity of the survey results. The respondent should feel that his or her answer fits one, and only one, possible category.

In the course of a telephone or personal interview, the respondent must understand the choices and then recall the one that applies to him or her. The number of choices in closed-ended questions for these interviews should not exceed five or six. Pretesting questions helps to ensure that the categories are clear, exhaustive, and mutually exclusive. If any interpretation problems are going to arise, the pretest stage is the time to discover them.

Closed-ended questions may have several types of response formats. The simplest and often the most appropriate set consists of *yes, no,* and *don't know.* For questions that require more options, investigators can choose partially closed-ended questions, closed-ended questions with ordered response choices, and closed-ended questions with unordered response choices. A *partially closed-ended* question allows the respondent to enter a response not listed by the researcher. The most probable choices are listed, but choices such as *other* and *don't know* are included as well. Researchers should use this structure when they can think of the probable responses but may be unsure about the exhaustiveness of the options. For instance, an item such as "Please circle the number next to the one city service you think needs the most improvement" may list several services as well as an "other" choice with a blank space next to it (see question 3a in Figure 4.4 for another example).

Partially closed-ended questions should not be employed as escape valves for poorly crafted response sets, and "other" options should not be appended to every closed-ended question. They should be included only when the researcher can identify the most likely responses but needs to measure the diversity that exists beyond those choices. Researchers should be aware that most people will not take the time to write in their choices if they do not appear on the list provided (Schwarz & Hippler, 1991).

Closed-ended questions with ordered choices are especially well suited for measuring questions about attitudes, beliefs, or behaviors. Responses to questions of this type often combine to form a multiple-item index to measure some concept important to the study. Examples are "public safety," "service satisfaction," or "civic-mindedness." The answer choices are a gradation of a dimension of some belief, behavior, or attitude. An "agree-disagree" response set measures opinions about specific statements. Evaluative questions may employ other types of ratings, such as "good," "fair," and "poor." Figure 4.2 presents examples of closed-ended questions with ordered choices.

Closed-ended questions with unordered response choices do not limit responses to gradations of a single concept. The unordered response structure is suitable for acquiring information on opinions, beliefs, behaviors, or attributes. The responses can help the researcher to establish priorities or to rank alternatives. Occasionally, the researcher may need to have the respondent "circle all that apply" in a list. In coding these, each choice is considered to be a distinct variable and is designated 1 if selected and 0 if not chosen. Figure 4.2 also illustrates examples of unordered response sets.

Choosing the Question Type

The key factors the researcher should review in deciding how to structure a particular question are as follows:

- The objectives of the survey and the types of information needed
- The knowledge or information the researcher and respondents have about the topic

Ordered choices:

For a telephone survey:
1. Are you inclined to agree or disagree with the following statement: "For the local taxes that I pay, the services provided by the city are a good bargain." Would you say that you:

>   1   STRONGLY DISAGREE
>   2   DISAGREE
>   3   NEITHER DISAGREE NOR AGREE
>   4   AGREE
>   5   STRONGLY AGREE

2. How would you rate the job performed by the public service department with respect to the timely removal of brush and leaves in your neighborhood? Would you say that it is:

>   1   POOR
>   2   FAIR
>   3   GOOD
>   4   NOT SURE/DON'T KNOW

Unordered choices:

1. Which of the following best describes the type of structure in which you reside?

>   1   SINGLE FAMILY
>   2   DUPLEX
>   3   APARTMENT IN BUILDING WITH 3 OR 4 UNITS
>   4   APARTMENT IN BUILDING WITH MORE THAN 4 UNITS
>   5   MOBILE HOME

2. Who do you think is **most** responsible for the success of the riverfront redevelopment project?

>   1   MAYOR
>   2   CITY COUNCIL
>   3   CITY PLANNERS
>   4   CHAMBER OF COMMERCE

3. Some problems in our city are listed below. Please rank these from 1 to 5, with 1 being *most* critical to 5 being *least* critical.

>   ____   TRASH ON CITY STREETS
>   ____   VIOLENCE IN THE PUBLIC SCHOOLS
>   ____   GRAFFITI ON BUILDINGS AND WALKWAYS
>   ____   LACK OF SHOPPING FACILITIES
>   ____   LACK OF AFFORDABLE HOUSING

Figure 4.2. Closed-Ended Questions With Ordered and Unordered Choices

-   How motivated respondents may be to communicate their experiences and thoughts
-   The level of measurement of the variable and the type of data analysis planned

Closed-ended questions are less demanding for respondents than are open-ended questions, and they typically constitute 90 to 95% of all questions in an instrument. When crafting these questions, the researcher has to be careful to avoid omitting an important choice or fashioning a response set that does not correspond to how or what respondents think. If the options presented are not exhaustive or mutually exclusive, respondents will be frustrated and response rates will decline. Clear, concise, and unambiguous closed-ended questions with exhaustive and exclusive answer choices are rewarded with higher response rates.

Open-ended questions are easier to write, but they present a more challenging free-recall task for respondents. They require more time and effort both for the respondent to complete and for the researcher to code. The judicious use of open-ended questions, however, may be highly informative, especially when the researcher is uncertain about the exhaustiveness of response choices. Open-ended questions offer respondents the opportunity to express their views or thoughts in their own words. People generally will respond to open-ended questions if they concern something they care about. In some cases, placing an open-ended question near the beginning of the questionnaire or telephone interview can help to establish a "consulting" tone for the remainder of the questionnaire or interview.

Open-ended questions are often the best choice when the investigator is interested in the salience of an issue, the order in which issues are recalled, or the proportions of respondents who recall particular issues without any prompting from a list of options. Closed formats, on the other hand, may remind respondents of alternatives that they otherwise may not have considered and are appropriate when the investigator desires to evaluate a larger set of specific items, to determine the intensity of opinions, or to assess the *relative* importance of choices. Table 4.1 summarizes the major attributes of the different question formats.

Avoiding Bias in Questionnaire Design

Bias exists whenever some feature of the survey instrument or interview process leads to a response that is not a genuine measure of the respondent's true opinion, attitude, belief, or attribute. Bias may occur in the instructions, question wording, question order, response choices, or the format of the instrument. Sometimes a guess about what people think can cause fewer problems than a biased survey whose thin scientific veneer misleads decision makers.

TABLE 4.1 The Merits of Open-Ended and Closed-Ended Questions

Question Type	Applications
Open-ended	Allows respondents to answer in their own words on topics that interest them and on which they have information. Especially useful for exploratory research questions that need to probe people's preferences, priorities, and positions. Appropriate when mutually exclusive and exhaustive response choices are difficult to devise or when such a list greatly increases the complexity of a question.
Partially closed-ended	The most probable or likely choices are presented but the list cannot be exhaustive because there is reason to suspect that opinion diversity exists among a small segment of the population. This question type permits respondents to offer their own answers. Because few persons usually select this option, a large number of responses to the "other" choice may suggest a defective response set.
Closed-ended with ordered choices	Especially useful for determining frequency of participation, intensity of feeling, or degree of involvement or contact. A scale that represents a gradation of a single concept distinguishes this question type. This format is especially useful for a series of attitude and belief questions.
Closed-ended with unordered choices	Used to help establish priorities, decide on alternative policies, or enumerate behaviors as long as the choices are exhaustive and mutually exclusive.

Instrumentation bias refers to defects in the way instructions, questions, or response choices are expressed or organized. Some of the most common sources of instrumentation bias are unclear or arcane vocabulary, poor grammar, excessively specific and demanding questions, double-barreled and loaded questions, unbalanced or overlapping response choices, and reliance on a single question to measure complex concepts. Interviewers may also introduce bias, through voice inflection that suggests preferred responses or by inconsistently phrasing questions. Interviewers must be thoroughly familiar with the survey protocol and sensitive to the importance of their being courteous, tactful, consistent, and helpful.

Sometimes the wording or format of a questionnaire can lead to *acquiescence response set bias.* This is the tendency for people to answer questions in a specific direction (either positive or negative). Respondents may "agree" with the first few questions about the desirability of reducing the size of government, for example, and then respond with or mark the same answer choice on the assumption that this choice applies to the rest of the questions that deal with smaller government or reduced spending. Respondents are quickly bored when they encounter too many questions with the same format, and they may superficially scan for answers they think apply, to end the ordeal quickly.

Singleton, Straits, and Straits (1993) suggest that one way to avoid acquiescence response set bias is to steer clear of the Likert scale format (the agree-disagree index) in favor of explicit response choices. Accordingly, the investigator may phrase a question in this format:

> Which of the following statements most closely reflects *your* opinion about the sales tax on food?
> 1 The sales tax on food should be abolished.
> 2 The sales tax on food should not be abolished.
> 3 Not sure/don't know.

Theoretically, a researcher can detect acquiescence response bias if the instrument has two different questions on the same topic. For example, at one point, the following question may be asked: "Some state legislators propose to abolish the state sales tax on food. Would you favor or oppose removal of the state sales tax on food?" Then, later in the survey, respondents are asked whether they agree or disagree with this statement: "The state sales tax on food should be abolished." If substantively different answers are given, the instrument may be biased. A distinct drawback to this strategy is that it takes up valuable time or space and annoys people who may feel their time is being wasted by survey sponsors who ask redundant questions. A better strategy is for the survey designer to write *interesting* questions in the first place and to vary the response choices for items in a series. Use of both questions and statements to measure variables is less monotonous.

Similarly, *straight-line response set bias* may occur when a long series of questions or statements with identical answer choices appears on a page. Use of the same "agree-disagree" scale for a long list of items is a recipe for disaster. A respondent may mark the first few items accurately, find the process boring, and speed through the rest of the instrument by marking the same answer for subsequent statements. In mail surveys this response is sometimes recognizable when a respondent marks a large circle around or a line through the same response choice in the series. Varying the arrangement, structure, and format of questions, and selecting different types of questions, eliminates straight-line response set bias.

Social desirability bias occurs when respondents are unwilling to admit or to report accurately various behaviors or opinions because these are not considered to be socially acceptable. The challenge for the researcher is to ask questions about socially sensitive issues in ways that elicit honest answers. Some people are reluctant to report their actual behaviors or opinions because they vary from socially acceptable or politically correct norms. The fear of being thought of as extreme, unpatriotic, indolent, or just plain stupid motivates people to avoid or to respond differently to various "mom and apple pie" issues, such as voting, recycling, environmental protection, child restraint seat use, and consumption of substances or foods known to cause health problems. Blunt questions on sensitive topics or issues embarrass people, and rational people want to avoid this emotion.

Social desirability bias can occur for any practice, behavior, or attitude that "conforms to the dominant belief patterns among groups to which the respondent feels some identification or allegiance" (Dillman, 1978, p. 62). Dillman (1978) suggests that this problem is most acute for personal interviews, affects telephone interviews occasionally, and is a less critical concern for impersonal mail surveys. Regardless of the method of contact, the researcher should always try to frame questions so that they will elicit undistorted, honest responses. The following are some examples of unnecessarily blunt questions that invite social desirability bias:

- Did you vote in the last mayoral election?
- About how many hours of television per day do you allow your elementary school child to view?
- Did you attend the last scheduled PTA meeting on the new special education programs offered in the Wildwood Elementary School?
- How much money did you make last year?
- Have you ever taken office supplies home with you?

Questions on sensitive topics should be phrased so that they are easy for respondents to answer truthfully. Weisberg, Krosnick, and Bowen (1989) suggest that questions about voting behavior, for example, can be phrased to assure people that nonvoting is reasonable, as in the following question:

In talking to people about the last city election, we found that some people were not able to vote because they weren't registered, were sick, or just didn't have the time. How about you—did you vote in the last city election? (p. 70)

Likewise, accurate information about parental attendance at a socially desirable event might be obtained by this question:

These days parents have many responsibilities and demands on their time and cannot always attend every school meeting. Did you attend the May meeting of the PTA on the new special education programs?

Employees can be asked, "How often, if at all, do you bring work home from the office?" "Do you normally use computer disks [printing paper, etc.] from the office for this homework?"

Response choices that offer *ranges* for sensitive attribute questions (income or age, for instance) are less intrusive and threatening. More people will answer frankly when asked about their annual household income if their choices are offered as ranges of dollar amounts. Likewise, some people are reluctant to report their exact ages, but they will check an age range (for example, 40-45) or report the year in which they were born.

Composing Questions and Response Choices

The central issue is how to formulate unbiased open- or closed-ended questions that will get good-quality responses. Scholars have wrestled with this issue ever since systematic public opinion polling began in 1935 (see, e.g., Belson, 1986; Biemer, Groves, Lyberg, Mathiowetz, & Sudman, 1991; Blankenship, 1940; Bradburn & Sudman, 1991; Payne, 1951; Schuman & Presser, 1981; Sudman & Bradburn, 1974). Although these studies have advanced our understanding of the survey process, two conclusions are evident: First, there is no formula for writing perfect questions and designing a flawless questionnaire; second, the survey method is an incredibly complex activity about which there is still much that we do not know. Our understanding of the social and cognitive processes that affect responses is still in its infancy.

Writing questions places dual demands on the researcher: First, questions must be unambiguous and must adequately measure what the researcher wants to measure; second, the questions must be understood to mean what the researcher intends them to mean by complete strangers who agree to engage in a voluntary social exchange. This exchange between researcher and respondent occurs within the larger context of "social norms governing relations between strangers, general canons of politeness, and ways of treating strangers" (Bradburn & Sudman, 1991, p. 31). Too often, researchers construct questions that make perfect sense to them, but that are misunderstood or misinterpreted by some respondents. To compound this error, researchers often pay too little attention to ways in which they can increase voluntary participation and make the interview a more pleasant experience for the respondent.

The challenge for the researcher, a daunting one indeed, is to write clear, unambiguous questions that are not so long and complex as to create additional problems of their own. This tension between specificity and simplicity is inherent to the task. A number of scholars have offered guidelines that can help survey designers to craft questions that strike a reasonable balance between these two values (see, e.g., Converse & Presser, 1986; Dillman, 1978; Oppenheim, 1992; Rubenstein, 1995; Weisberg et al., 1989). These prescriptions, founded on common sense and refined by experience, can help investigators avoid egregious flaws in their wording of questions and responses. Later in this section I will review and illustrate these guidelines, but first I want to discuss an approach to the question-answer exchange relationship that can help to encourage participation and reduce the "costs" of respondents' participation.

POSITIVE INDUCEMENTS

Every survey is unique in several respects, and what really happens in the social exchange process varies among surveys. An approach to question wording and instrument design that I have found to work well consistently, regardless of the type or purpose of the survey, consists of two basic practices: a *reality check* and a *consideration check*.

First, the researcher should try to imagine being "in the respondent's shoes" and hearing (or reading) each question for the first time. Every question and draft of the instrument should be viewed from this perspective, with an eye to answering the question, How can this be misunderstood by or bore the respondent? If the researcher can conceive of *any* way someone might misinterpret, misconstrue, or take offense at a question, then the chances are fairly good that some people in the target population also will have this reaction. Removing defects in the language and structure of questions that might produce inconsistent responses or deter participation is a fundamental reality check.

The second practice is for the researcher to remember that the entire survey enterprise depends on inducing people to volunteer their time to perform what amounts to doing him or her a favor. The golden rule of survey design is to show the respondent consistent consideration and respect in every aspect of the instrument, from the cover letter or introductory spiel to the expression of appreciation at closure. Obtaining voluntary cooperation requires the practice of survey etiquette. The language used should be polite, respectful, and understood by people in the target population. The instrument itself should be attractive, clear, and easy to follow. The cover letter or introduction should explain clearly what the investigator or interviewer is doing and why, as well as why the respondent's help is needed. A polite request for the individual's help, an *accurate* estimate of how long the process will take, and an acknowledgment of the person's permission to proceed are good ways to build rapport. The language of the instrument should be free of jargon, all words should be spelled correctly, and the vocabulary should be appropriate for the mean level of educational attainment of the target population. Transition statements should introduce batteries of questions and perhaps briefly describe why it is important for the respondent to take the time to answer them.

Packing questions densely onto a page creates the perception in the respondent that all the researcher cares about is saving a little money on paper; this communicates little regard for the respondent's task burden. Adequate white space between the vertical ordering of questions and response choices both improves their appearance and facilitates a sense of progress as items are completed. Questions that are neat, orderly, and piloted by directions are easier to follow. Consistent vertical orientation of items makes the product visually smoother. The use of a consistent method for marking responses on similar items—whether checking, circling, or underlining—helps to minimize later data entry errors.

In the interview process, respect and consideration for the respondent often make the difference between a hang-up or door slam and a successfully completed interview. Courteous, polite callers who are thoroughly familiar with the instrument and who have good listening skills can guide respondents through questions quickly, with a minimum of inconvenience or frustration. Interjecting a "please" or "would you mind" where appropriate is a simple act of courtesy that makes people feel they are being treated with civility and respect.

This approach to the social exchange that attends survey implementation requires a conscious effort to attend to all of the details that cumulatively shape a respondent's decision to participate. Building rapport founded on respect and consideration for the individual results in a qualitatively different kind of survey process that should help to increase the quantity of completed surveys. This approach is now distinctive in an era rife with obnoxious and relentless telemarketers and mail questionnaire prize scams.

The researcher may also want to offer a material inducement to potential respondents, such as a copy of the executive summary of the survey results. The idea is to offer something more than just a psychic reward for

Example of an unrevised original

In my pursuit of scholarly research: (Circle the number most appropriate, where 1 = strongly disagree and 10 = strongly agree.) Please skip question if it does not apply to you.

44. I have developed a plan for my research activities and success.
    Strongly Disagree   1   2   3   4   5   6   7   8   9   10   *Strongly Agree*

45. Most successful researchers have a plan for personal objectives and success, which they monitor and update as conditions change.
    Strongly Disagree   1   2   3   4   5   6   7   8   9   10   *Strongly Agree*

46. Because of the serendipitous nature of research, scholarly achievements and success are mainly beyond the control of the researcher.
    Strongly Disagree   1   2   3   4   5   6   7   8   9   10   *Strongly Agree*

47. I choose research topics based on likely availability of funds.
    Strongly Disagree   1   2   3   4   5   6   7   8   9   10   *Strongly Agree*

48. Whether or not specific research enhances one's career largely depends on its timing and trendiness.
    Strongly Disagree   1   2   3   4   5   6   7   8   9   10   *Strongly Agree*

49. Before sending an article to a journal, I carefully research what types of articles and methodologies have been published in that journal previously.
    Strongly Disagree   1   2   3   4   5   6   7   8   9   10   *Strongly Agree*

50. I choose research topics primarily based on my professional interests.
    Strongly Disagree   1   2   3   4   5   6   7   8   9   10   *Strongly Agree*

51. Before applying for a grant, I often lay the groundwork by checking with the funding sources and/or those sponsoring the RFP.
    Strongly Disagree   1   2   3   4   5   6   7   8   9   10   *Strongly Agree*

52. I think quantity and number of publications is an important indicator of research success.
    Strongly Disagree   1   2   3   4   5   6   7   8   9   10   *Strongly Agree*

This same format continues for two more pages, through question 83.

Critique

Several questions are arguably double-barreled, use redundant or unnecessary words, and pertain to topics that are apparently unrelated to the subject of the pursuit of scholarly research. Questions 45 and 48, for example, ask for information that no one person possesses. Use of the same response set is fatiguing and invites response set bias. It is also inappropriate for some of the questions. No labels or definitions are offered for values 2 through 9 in the scale. A respondent must guess whether a 5 is a neutral response or a "neither disagree nor agree" choice.

The reliance on a 10-point Likert-type scale decreases the reliability of the instrument. How likely is it that you would choose the same number for an item two days hence? Listing the response choices horizontally is visually difficult to follow and increases the perceived task burden. Use of vertical question flow and white space reduces the perceived task burden.

Figure 4.3. Revising a Mail Questionnaire

participation. Tangible inducements may also include coupons or discounts for various services or programs. These are limited only by the imagination and the budget of the survey sponsors.

It is always easier to critique someone else's attempt to compose questions on complex subjects than it is to create questions that conform to all of the

Possible revisions

A transition statement:

The following questions will help us to understand how you approach your research and what *you* think it means to be a "successful" researcher. (Please circle the numbers to the left of your answers.)

1. Have you prepared a formal plan to help you accomplish your research objectives?

   1 NO
   2 YES

2. Before you submit a manuscript to a journal, is it your practice to determine whether that journal has published articles on topics similar to yours?

   1 NO
   2 YES

3. Do you review the methodological approaches employed by previous authors before you submit a manuscript to a particular journal?

   1 NO
   2 YES

4. Which statement *best* describes your perspective on what accounts for research publication success? (Circle the number next to your choice.)

   1 Whether a journal accepts my manuscript is primarily a matter of serendipity.
   2 Which reviewers the editor decides to send my manuscript to primarily determines whether it will be published.
   3 If I submit a manuscript on a currently popular topic in my discipline, it is much more likely to be published.
   4 Whether my manuscript is accepted for publication depends mostly on whether I am able to incorporate sophisticated statistical methods that are currently in vogue.

5. If you *had* to choose *one* of the following, which do you think is a *better* indicator of a scholar's "research success" over a 10-year period?

   1 Publication of 5 articles in the premier quality journal in your field.
   2 Publication of 10 articles in several journals of good quality in your field.
   3 Publication of three books of original research by an academic press.

Figure 4.3. Continued

guidelines offered so far in this chapter. This is why peer review and pretesting are so important. Survey designers need practice to be able to recognize all of the possible defects that a draft instrument may contain. One of the best ways to learn how to incorporate these guidelines in one's own work is to critique the many surveys that one receives in the mail. For example, Figure 4.3 reproduces as closely as possible a small portion of a questionnaire sent to coordinators of graduate programs in public administration, along with a critique of some of the instrument's major problems and some suggestions for improvements.

Composition Standards

Simplicity, brevity, clarity, coherence, consistency, and symmetry are the main considerations in writing good questions and response sets. Some word processing programs (Microsoft Word®, for instance) can calculate a Flesch Reading Ease formula, which computes readability based on the number of syllables per word and the average number of words per sentence, and assigns scores ranging from 0 to 100. Standard writing scores average between 60 and 70. The higher the score, the larger the number of people who can readily understand the material. Such a tool can be useful as the researcher begins editorial revisions on the survey instrument.

SIMPLICITY VERSUS SPECIFICITY

Relatively short questions (with fewer than 20 words) are especially important for telephone interviews, because they minimize the task burden of the respondent. Lengthy, complex sentences and ideas should be broken up into shorter ones. Clear, concise sentences also have specific time references. If a technical term is essential, it should be defined so that no ambiguity exists about its meaning. Also, the researcher should consider asking two or three questions, instead of one, to measure the distinct elements of a complex process or concept.

For example, a manager may want to know what employees think about a new performance appraisal system. She may begin with the question, "Do you think your supervisor's judgment is affected by recency errors since the new BARS was devised for your position?" Complexity rather than length is the main concern here. Even a knowledgeable employee may not be sure that BARS is an acronym for *behaviorally anchored rating scale* or that *recency error* refers to judgments based only on recent behaviors rather than overall performance since the last evaluation. Also, will all employees know precisely *when* the new appraisal system was devised? Three questions that employ clear concepts and a common reference period might improve the quality of responses. Figure 4.4 illustrates these improvements.

The need for specificity often requires that a researcher include more complex sentences or more questions. Several drafts *and* pretesting are necessary to achieve the best balance for a particular information objective. The fruits of this toil are questions that are less likely to be misinterpreted. Examples of some first-draft efforts and improved revisions are presented in Figure 4.4.

Unnecessarily complex and difficult:

1. Do you think your supervisor's judgment is affected by recency errors since the new BARS was devised for your position?

Improved:

1a. Since July 1997, your supervisor has used a new rating scale to evaluate your job performance. What do you think about the fairness of this new rating scale compared to the old appraisal system? Would you say that it is

     1 WORSE
     2 ABOUT THE SAME
     3 BETTER

1b. In thinking about your last job evaluation, do you believe your supervisor *accurately* appraised your performance?

     1 NO
     2 YES
     3 NOT SURE/DON'T KNOW

     1c. Please describe why you think your supervisor did **not** accurately appraise your job performance in the last evaluation.

Unnecessarily complex and difficult:

2. Considering your company's strategic plan for growth and increased market share, how would you expect your industrial sector's generation of hazardous wastes to change during the next five years?   [Open-ended]

Improved:

2. By the year 2000, do you expect the hazardous waste generated at your plant to decrease, stay the same, or increase?

     1 DECREASE
     2 STAY THE SAME
     3 INCREASE

Figure 4.4. Improving Question Clarity

CLARITY

A researcher should not expect too much from a single question. Questions with compound subjects risk being *double-barreled*; that is, they really ask two or more questions but limit respondents to single answers. Asking double-barreled questions is among the most common errors in survey design. The unrevised Question 3 in Figure 4.4 provides an example.

Unnecessarily complex and difficult:

3. Does your household recycle PET and HDPE plastics at the community drop-off collection center?

    1 NO
    2 YES
    3 NOT SURE/DON'T KNOW

Improved:

3. Do you recycle any materials at the community drop-off collection center?

    1 NO
    2 YES
    3 NOT SURE/DON'T KNOW

    3a. If YES, which of the following materials do you usually take to the center? (Please circle the numbers for all that apply.)

        1 Plastic milk bottles or jugs
        2 Plastic soda bottles
        3 Newspaper
        4 Aluminum cans
        5 Clear glass containers
        6 Other (please specify)_____

Figure 4.4. Continued

Figure 4.5 offers additional illustrations; for instance, Question 1 in Figure 4.5 incorporates several distinct issues. It also is biased because it implies that higher teacher salaries and less spending on athletics affect school quality. As a rule, investigators should avoid *false assumptions* about linkages between concepts. Separate questions are appropriate for measuring support for more spending for teacher salaries and support for less spending on athletics and after-school programs. School quality also needs to be defined. "Better school quality" is an output from an educational system and does not necessarily equate with an input such as higher teacher salaries. Perhaps improvement in reading scores on standardized tests is a better measure. Unambiguous measures of distinct elements improve question clarity.

In Question 2 in Figure 4.5, more than one response choice can apply to the respondent or to family members. In addition, some people might think of "family" as broader than just those living in the immediate household, so validity problems arise with the use of this term. Again, there is a dubious assumption that the respondent has accurate information about the experiences of other family members. One solution would be to ask two questions and to substitute *household* for *family.*

Researchers should be careful to scrutinize any question that contains the word *and* to determine whether or not it is a double-barreled question.

Double-barreled and leading:
1. Do you favor increasing the quality of our public school system by raising the property tax to give teachers higher salaries and to offer students more after-school learning programs?

      1 FAVOR
      2 OPPOSE
      3 DON'T KNOW/ NOT SURE

Revised:
1a. Would you support a local property tax increase to give teachers in the district's public schools a 10% salary raise?

      1 NO
      2 YES
      3 DON'T KNOW/ NOT SURE

1b. Would you support a local property tax increase to expand after-school learning programs for children in public school grades 1 through 6?

      1 NO
      2 YES
      3 DON'T KNOW/ NOT SURE

1c. Do you think how much money teachers make has any impact on their students' performance on standardized reading tests?

      1 NO
      2 YES
      3 DON'T KNOW/ NOT SURE

A double-barreled question:
2. How many times were you or a member of your family a victim of a crime during 1995?

      1 NOT AT ALL
      2 ONCE
      3 TWICE
      4 THREE OR MORE TIMES
      5 DON'T KNOW/NOT SURE

Revised:
2a. Were you a victim of a crime at any time during 1995 in the city of Mesa?

      1 NO
      2 YES

      2b. If YES, did the Mesa police apprehend anyone suspected of committing the crime against you?

          1 NO
          2 YES
          3 DON'T KNOW/NOT SURE

Figure 4.5. Fixing Double-Barreled Questions

Concepts should be clear and distinct. Separate questions are appropriate if their importance to the survey is justified. Question clarity suffers when the investigator assumes that respondents know as much about a topic as he or she does. Whenever any doubt exists about respondents' knowledge

A double-barreled question:
3. Was the police officer in your most recent contact helpful and courteous?

> 1 NO
> 2 YES
> 3 DON'T KNOW/NOT SURE

Revised:
3a. Was the police officer in your most recent contact helpful to you?

> 1 NO
> 2 YES
> 3 DON'T KNOW/NOT SURE

3b. Was the police officer in your most recent contact courteous to you?
> 1 NO
> 2 YES
> 3 DON'T KNOW/NOT SURE

Figure 4.5. Continued

about a topic, the researcher should insert a screen question to determine respondents' familiarity with it. This practice makes it clear that an answer is not required if respondents have no information about it. It also helps to distinguish genuine attitudes from nonattitudes. An alternative to the use of a screen question is to preface a question with a neutral explanation.

Double negatives mar question clarity. Survey designers should avoid phrasing questions in negative terms, such as *"Don't* you agree that the property tax should *not* be increased this year to cover the projected deficit?" Such questions are easily misinterpreted, and respondents may have different perceptions of what yes and no responses mean. The word *agree* in this example also suggests that people *should* agree. A good practice is to *balance* the language in attitudinal questions and to use *nondirectional* language whenever possible. Phrases such as *agree or disagree, favor or oppose,* and *satisfied or dissatisfied* balance a question. Nondirectional language directs attention to clear, mutually exclusive choices, for example, "Which option do you think the city should employ to avoid the projected deficit at the end of the year?"

Consistency in question interpretation is the critical objective. *Unclear* or *unstated criteria* open a question to misinterpretation. Questions with multiple interpretations are not valid measures. For example, "How important is it that the state maintain the existing income tax rate?" is a question that might mean different things to different people. Many citizens can be counted on to think in terms of their own monetary circumstances and answer with the choice "very unimportant," because they would like to see the tax rate reduced. Industrialists might think the current rate is good for business and so may answer with "very important." Still others may believe it is important to increase the tax rate to fund education at a higher level and thus may select "very unimportant." An improved question with more explicit criteria would be as follows: "Do *you* think the state should increase, keep the same, or decrease the existing 6% tax on personal income?" An open-ended follow-up question may ask *why* the respondent holds this opinion. To maximize question clarity, the researcher must have a clear focus on what information interests the survey sponsors.

Unfortunately, there is no dictionary of "commonly understood survey terms." Payne (1951) offers a "Rogue's Gallery of Problem Words" (pp. 158-176) that is worth consulting, but the best strategy for a researcher to employ after making his or her best effort to draft clear questions is to pretest them on a group from the target population.

AVOIDING BIASED TERMS AND LOADED QUESTIONS

Biased questions lead people to respond in ways that do not reflect their true opinions or attitudes about an issue. Survey designers should excise any terms, phrases, and clichés that appeal to emotions or that evoke visceral responses. Examples of terms laden with emotional or ideological baggage include *cops, bureaucrats, government planning, justice, welfare, dump, liberal,* and *conservative.*

Leading questions suggest that some answers are more acceptable than others, for example, "Do you favor spending more money to make our streets safer by expanding the local jailhouse to hold a larger number of drunk drivers being convicted in our city?" This is obviously a biased, double-barreled, and leading question. Rhetoric, pretentiousness, and demagoguery are not consistent with objective question composition. The researcher should strive to be as straightforward as possible about what he or she wants to know. An improved version of the preceding question might read: "Do you favor or oppose a 2 cent increase in the property tax rate to build additional cells in the local jail?"

Questions should be nondirectional; that is, nothing in the language should suggest, even subconsciously, the desirability of one response over another. A subtle kind of misleading question is illustrated by the following: "Would you consider voting for someone other than Bill Clinton for president if the 1996 election were held today?" Well, who would not at least *consider* voting for someone else? Opinions on this question are likely to differ markedly from a more straightforward query: "If the 1996 election were held today, how likely is it that you would vote for Bill Clinton for president?" The response choices could be "not at all likely," "somewhat likely," and "very likely."

TIME REFERENCES

An explicit *time frame* minimizes the recall burden for respondents and facilitates interpretation of responses. A mail survey typically requires 6 to 8 weeks to complete. Use of an imprecise time period in a question, such as "the past 2 months," means that those who answer the first mailing and those who respond to the third will have different time frames in mind. Specific, recent time references are easier for people to recollect accurately.

The memory burden on respondents is less demanding if response choices include ranges. Instead of asking an open-ended question such as "How many times did you use the city trolley system during 1997?" the researcher can insert "About" at the beginning of the question and then offer frequency ranges, such as "not at all," "fewer than 5 times," "from 6 to 10 times," and "more than 10 times." Ranges are not as precise as interval-level data, but they reduce the respondent's recall burden and increase the reliability of responses.

Questions should not demand extremely precise recollection or calculation by the respondent. A question such as "What is your mean net family income per week?" is difficult for most people to answer, because few people think in those terms. Instead, the question should ask for total household income for a particular year. The researcher can always calculate an average monthly income later in the data analysis stage.

SYMMETRY

Balanced response choices improve symmetry and question objectivity. Response sets should have equal numbers of negative and positive choices and, where appropriate, a middle category for those who have no opinion. Unbalanced rating scales seem to appeal to fast-food chain marketing departments, whose customer evaluation cards typically offer only "excellent," "very good," "good," and "poor" choices, so that three of the four options are obviously positive. Unbiased response choices are always symmetrical and balanced. Figure 4.6 shows some questions with unsymmetrical and symmetrical response choices and suggests other possible balanced response sets.

Examples of unbalanced response choices:

1. How would you rate the food at Nebraska Bob's Raw Oyster Bar?

  1 ☐ EXCELLENT
  2 ☐ VERY GOOD
  3 ☐ GOOD
  4 ☐ FAIR

2. Overall, how satisfied are you with the quality of education in the county school system?

  1 ☐ VERY SATISFIED
  2 ☐ SATISFIED
  3 ☐ SOMEWHAT SATISFIED
  4 ☐ DISSATISFIED

Examples of balanced response choices:

1. How would you rate the overall quality of food that you ordered this evening at Che Rivera? (Please check one.)

  1 ☐ EXCELLENT
  2 ☐ GOOD
  3 ☐ AVERAGE
  4 ☐ POOR
  5 ☐ VERY POOR

2. Overall, how satisfied are you with the quality of education in the county school system? (Please check one.)

  1 ☐ VERY SATISFIED
  2 ☐ SATISFIED
  3 ☐ NEITHER SATISFIED NOR DISSATISFIED
  4 ☐ DISSATISFIED
  5 ☐ VERY DISSATISFIED

Examples of other balanced response sets:

excellent	increase	too much	strongly agree	good
good	stay the same	about right	agree	fair
neither good	decrease	too little	disagree	poor
nor poor			strongly disagree	
poor				
very poor				

  desirable
  somewhat desirable
  somewhat undesirable
  undesirable

Figure 4.6. Balancing Response Choices

Question Order for Mail Surveys

Question order affects responses in a variety of ways, only some of which are known to scholars. In between the gripping questions that lead off the questionnaire and the more sensitive items that bring up the rear, much can happen to shape responses in ways the researcher should *try* to anticipate. In particular, the investigator should consider how preceding questions might direct or influence answers to later questions. The objective is to order questions within topical sections so as not to bias later responses.

Question order should not create *priming effects* for later questions in a series. For example, the researcher should avoid asking a series of questions about local crime and perceived threats to public safety before asking the respondent to rank in order of importance a list of five problems, one of which is "the local crime rate." The respondent in such a situation will be sensitized to the crime issue and may rank it higher than he or she might have otherwise. A strategy to help rectify this problem is to use a *funnel sequence* for questions. When topics are already important to respondents, the researcher should start with *general* questions and then funnel to more specific ones. General rankings or ratings of various problems, goals, or programs before specific items on these topics minimize respondents' sensitization. This avoids the artificial elevation of a particular item in the mental response hierarchy of a respondent. For example, several questions about recycling followed by a question about what citizens can do to help their community will result in recycling being mentioned more frequently or ranked more highly than if this general ranking question preceded specific questions about this practice. When topics are not particularly stimulating, the researcher should start with specific questions to provide respondents with a frame of reference and then ask more general questions about the topic. This is often called an *inverted funnel sequence.*

There are always potential problems in obtaining consistent rankings and ratings of items in a series. Research in the fields of advertising and sociology suggests that some respondents assign more importance to items listed first in any series. Because the positions of items may affect their likelihood of being selected or endorsed, interviewers conducting personal or telephone interviews can be instructed to modify the order in which items are read. It is usually prohibitively expensive to print different versions of self-administered surveys, but items in such instruments can be presented in alphabetical order, or statements can be included that indicate the items are listed in random order.

The most sensitive questions in the instrument should be placed *at the ends* of their respective sections. Attribute and background questions usually make up the last section of the questionnaire, with the most sensitive questions, such as those concerning income, race, and political party identification, located at the end of this section. The rationale is to obtain responses to the most critical questions before the respondent gets turned off by queries on more sensitive subjects.

Constructing Indexes and Scales

A single question is insufficient for measuring complex concepts such as socioeconomic status, participation, freedom, quality of life, safety, service satisfaction, government responsiveness, business climate, fiscal stress, employee morale, knowledge, faithfulness, piety, and ideological orientation. Several questions are necessary to capture the multiple dimensions involved in such concepts. Multiple indicators of a concept provide more valid, reliable, and precise measures, and results are not affected as much by the wording of a single question. For example, if a researcher asks people what their socioeconomic status is, he or she is likely to be met with blank stares. A better way to ascertain this information is to create a composite measure by asking questions that respondents can answer about the three variables researchers typically use to define this concept: income, education, and occupation.

Many composite measures already exist, and some are useful for the kinds of surveys conducted by public administrators. As I have noted, researchers should always review the published research on the topics in which they are interested, as well as the indexes constructed by national polling organizations. However, advances in our understanding of social and political phenomena often stem from better, more innovative measures of complex concepts. If a researcher can create an index that is more appropriate than those used in the past for the information needs of a particular project, he or she should not feel shackled by those already published.

An *index* is a composite measure of scores on individual items that relate to a specific concept. Indexes abound in daily administrative life. The FBI's Uniform Crime Index, the Department of Labor's Consumer Price Index, the Dow-Jones Index of stocks, the "misery index" (popular near election time), and even a student's grade point average are examples of composite measures of variables that attempt to measure complex concepts.

Constructing an index is a straightforward task that involves the following steps:

- Define the concept clearly.
- Choose the indicators for the concept.

- Combine the items to create an index.
- Weight items in the index (optional).

To define a concept means to specify its key elements or components. Social scientists derive these from theories, practice, and previous research. A concept is measured by indicators or index items that serve as the operational definition of the concept. Indicators that are logically related to a concept have *face validity,* or a commonsense linkage with the concept. The index is constructed by assigning a range of possible scores to each item. The sum of the scores on the individual items is the composite index score for a case. Weights can be assigned to indicators that are more important or influential for an index of a concept.

For example, there are several indicators of a "downtown's image." Questions can measure an individual's positive or negative orientation to each indicator. Adverbs modify the intensity of opinions. Respondents may be "very satisfied," "satisfied," "neither satisfied nor dissatisfied," "dissatisfied," or "very dissatisfied" with items. Similarly, they can be asked whether they agree or disagree with statements about each item. Possible indicators of a downtown's image are the cleanliness of sidewalks and streets, accessibility, traffic congestion, the appearance of storefronts, the aesthetics of signs and buildings, the convenience of parking, and a sense of personal safety when walking downtown. Each indicator should add something to a person's composite image of a downtown. Figure 4.7 gives examples of a few of the questions that measure these indicators.

The items of an index are chosen carefully to represent the most important dimensions of a concept. Balanced questions or statements control response set bias. Changing the "direction" of items forces respondents to consider their answers more carefully. In Figure 4.7, Questions 1 and 3 are positive statements, whereas Questions 2 and 4 are negative. A higher value is assigned if a respondent agrees with 1 and 3, and a lower value is assigned if the respondent agrees with 2 and 4. This coding scheme assigns higher scores to more favorable attitudes about the downtown's image. Cases with a less favorable image will have lower scores. Alternatively, the values for a statement can be recoded in the data analysis stage rather than appear in reverse order as shown here for purposes of illustration.

How many response choices are appropriate for an item in an index? It is desirable to capture the full range of opinions or orientations on a subject, but there is also a need to have a sufficient number of cases in each response to make analysis of the results meaningful. A large number of response choices make the questionnaire more complex and time-consuming. The

Instructions: Please circle the number next to your answer to each question.

1. I am usually able to find a parking space in a convenient location when I travel downtown.

    1   STRONGLY DISAGREE
    2   DISAGREE
    3   NEITHER AGREE NOR DISAGREE
    4   AGREE
    5   STRONGLY AGREE

2. The streets and sidewalks downtown are usually dirty and littered.

    5   STRONGLY DISAGREE
    4   DISAGREE
    3   NEITHER AGREE NOR DISAGREE
    2   AGREE
    1   STRONGLY AGREE

3. I feel safe when walking in the downtown area.

    1   STRONGLY DISAGREE
    2   DISAGREE
    3   NEITHER AGREE NOR DISAGREE
    4   AGREE
    5   STRONGLY AGREE

4. Most of the buildings that border Main Street appear to be run-down and poorly maintained.

    5   STRONGLY DISAGREE
    4   DISAGREE
    3   NEITHER AGREE NOR DISAGREE
    2   AGREE
    1   STRONGLY AGREE

Figure 4.7. Items in an Index for Perceptions of a Downtown's Image

compromise can be as straightforward as a yes or no response, or as complex as a five-part agree-disagree scale. Usually, fewer response options are preferred.

The researcher may decide that some indicators are more important than others and deserve more weight in the computation of the index. Normally, items will have equal weight unless there is some historical, theoretical, empirical, or other reason to believe that one or more of the items are significantly more important in shaping a person's standing or position on some index. An example is an index of a person's environmental activism. A monetary contribution to an interest group, for instance, might be weighted more heavily than just support for stricter air pollution control. In the survey's final report, the researcher should describe the reasons for the weighting of various items in the index.

For a simple additive index, each response to an item is assigned a value. The sum or the mean of the item values constitutes the index score. For example, a hypothetical measure of environmental activism might consist of four questions about membership in an environmental protection organization, the regular practice of solid waste recycling, monetary contributions to an environmental preservation cause, and participation in an organized demonstration about an environmental issue. The responses to each question (or variable) in the index may be coded as no = 0 and yes = 1, depending on whether or not the person checked any of the listed behaviors. Each case has a potential index score of 0, 1, 2, 3, or 4, depending on the number of items in which the respondent engaged. If the researcher considers participation in an organized demonstration to be a more important indicator of activism than the other activities listed, he or she could assign a yes response a weight of 2. The *score weight* products are then added to compute the index score. In this case, a score may range from 0 to 5.

What if a respondent does not answer all of the questions that form an index? How are these missing data handled? Nonresponses are coded 9 or 99, or any number other than the one for a legitimate answer. The frequency distributions indicate the extent of a missing data problem for each question. There are several strategies that researchers use to deal with missing data. If only a few cases have missing data, these cases may be excluded from the analysis. If one of the indicators in a scale has an extraordinarily large number of nonresponses, it can be excluded and a new operational definition of the concept presented. Another, less satisfactory, method is to compute the average score for a case on the questions that have been answered and then assign this mean to the unanswered question(s). Still another strategy is to assign the middle score or the mean score of an item to a case that has not answered the question(s). With large samples, the first strategy is preferred. For a survey with a small *n* or response, the exclusion of all cases with missing data may bias the findings. Regrettably, there is no highly satisfactory solution to the problem of missing data, but the methods listed above are in rough order of preference.

To validate an index, it is necessary to determine whether each of the items in it contributes to the explanatory power of the composite measure. *Item analysis* is the method used to ascertain whether each of the items is correlated with the composite measure or index score. In item analysis, the index score is the independent variable and the item is the dependent variable. A measure of association (described in Chapter 6) indicates whether an item is strongly associated with the index. If it is not correlated with the index, that item should be dropped from the composite measure. If the items all correlate strongly with the index, then it is a good measure of the concept.

A commonly used index is the *Likert scale*. This index, incorrectly termed a scale, presents respondents with statements about which they are asked to agree or disagree. Usually the choices consist of a five-part agreement scale, as illustrated in Figure 4.7. The items in an index are ordinal measures. In other words, they indicate "more or less" of something but not *precisely* how much between cases. The composite scores rank cases on a particular concept.

Technically, one should use only the statistics appropriate for the level of measurement of the data. In practice, some scholars use interval-level statistics for composite scores from Likert scales to compute means or correlations as part of the data analysis stage. Empirical purists reject this practice, but the debate about it continues. In practice, this means that some analysts assume that a score from an ordinal index is an interval-level measure. This practice is ill-advised, but if the researcher employs it, he or she should be very cautious about imputing any great policy significance to fine distinctions among respondents' "mean" scores.

Indexes can improve the accuracy and validity of the measurement of complex concepts, but researchers should avoid the overuse of Likert scales. Whenever possible, it is better to employ simple yes or no response choices, because these provide accurate and reliable measures of what people think about the various dimensions that constitute concepts.

Designing the Mail Questionnaire

The appearance of a mail questionnaire is especially important. The pages of the questionnaire should have plenty of white space to make it easier to read and to allow the respondent to follow the vertical flow of the questions. The goal is to make the questionnaire inviting, pleasing to the eye, and easy to complete. Concise instructions should accompany different types of questions, and transition statements should lead off each cognitively related group of questions. Several suggestions to help investigators prepare an appealing instrument are listed in Table 4.2. Figure 4.8 shows some hypothetical questions that conform to these criteria.

THE COVER LETTER

A good cover letter encourages participation, and a poor one does little to persuade respondents not to toss the questionnaire in the trash. Altruistic appeals for participation work, but the inducements discussed earlier, such as offering to send the respondent an executive summary, enhance the

TABLE 4.2 Guidelines for Constructing Mail Questionnaires

Never cram too many questions onto a page so that it looks dense and cluttered. This increases the respondent's perceived task burden.

Whenever possible, do not break a question between pages.

The instrument length generally should not exceed 12 page faces.

Lead off the instrument with an interesting, easy-to-answer question that is clearly related to the purpose of the survey as explained in the cover letter. An open-ended question asked early often helps to establish a consulting tone.

Vary the types of questions to avoid response set bias. Long series of "yes or no" and "agree or disagree" questions fatigue respondents and lower the rate of completed surveys.

Incorporate the coding scheme into the question response sets to facilitate data processing.

Provide sufficient space for the respondent to write answers to open-ended questions, but do not provide lines, as this may constrain any comments.

Use a legible type in an easily readable font size. Capitalization of response choices often helps to focus the interviewer's and respondent's attention on them.

Allow sufficient space between questions and response choices to minimize coding and data entry errors.

Establish a vertical flow for questions and response choices. This helps to prevent inadvertent omissions and facilitates the perception of making rapid progress through the questionnaire. This technique automatically creates white space on the instrument.

Group questions by topic and use transition statements between topics to enhance the flow and continuity of the questionnaire.

Place the most sensitive questions at the ends of their respective sections. Attribute and background questions should usually constitute the final section.

Always thank the respondent for taking the time to complete the questionnaire.

Always pretest the questionnaire on a small sample of the target population.

Always place identification numbers on the survey instruments to track responses. This practice is essential for the direction of follow-up mailings.

---

credibility of the social exchange. The cover letter should be printed on the official stationery of the organization responsible, to lend legitimacy to the survey. It should be signed (not signature stamped) by the official in charge of the project. People are more likely to respond to surveys conducted by organizations or persons they know about. Dillman (1978) offers several excellent suggestions for composing a cover letter; Table 4.3 summarizes these ideas, and Figures 4.9 and 4.10 provide examples of cover letters for first and second mailings.

THE MAIL QUESTIONNAIRE BOOKLET

Questionnaires prepared in booklet form are attractive and reduce the number of sheets needed. There are several options for preparing question-naire booklets, but some general recommendations include using paper

1. First, we would like to know what you think is the single *most* important problem facing the city. Please tell us in the space below what you think that most important problem is:

2. Considering the services that you receive, do you think that your city property taxes are:

   1 TOO LOW

   2 ABOUT RIGHT

   3 TOO HIGH

   4 DON'T KNOW or NOT SURE

3. Please take a few moments to rate the quality of each of the following city services. Please *circle* the number that corresponds to your rating of that service's overall quality.

Quality Rating

Service	Very Poor	Poor	Average	Good	Very Good	Not Sure/ Don't Know
Crime Control	1	2	3	4	5	6
Fire Protection	1	2	3	4	5	6
Pothole Patching	1	2	3	4	5	6
Garbage Collection	1	2	3	4	5	6

4. Some people say that on-street parking on Main Street downtown should be eliminated to improve traffic flow and reduce congestion. Other people say that on-street parking on Main Street should remain for the convenience of workers and shoppers downtown. How do you feel about this issue? (Please select the one choice that best fits your opinion.)

   1 On-street parking on Main Street downtown should be eliminated.
   2 On-street parking on Main Street downtown should not be eliminated.
   3 Don't know/Not sure

Figure 4.8. Mail Questionnaire Page Format

with at least some recycled content and printing the pages with a laser printer. High-quality photocopying on both sides of all pages reduces costs. Off-white, light blue, or light green paper enhances type legibility.

The designer can use a mock-up to determine how the page faces should be numbered so that they are in the correct order when the printed full-size pages are folded and stapled to form a booklet. For example, there are 12 page faces to be numbered if three sheets of paper are needed for all of the

TABLE 4.3 Guidelines for Composing a Cover Letter

The letter should be brief and concise; a length of three or four paragraphs is ideal.

The letter should be printed on official stationery, should be dated, and should be signed (not signature stamped) by the official responsible for the project.

Explain the purpose of the study in the first paragraph. Communicate the importance and utility of the study in the second paragraph. Assure the reader of the confidentiality of responses in the third paragraph. Thank the prospective respondent for taking a few minutes to help with the project in the final paragraph. Inclusion of a "deadline" for completion and return of the questionnaire is optional.

Avoid using worn-out phrases that may turn off respondents (e.g., "Enclosed is a questionnaire"; "This is a survey"; "I am conducting research"; "You are important to our study").

Do not inject bias either for or against particular officials, organizations, or issues.

If the budget permits, offer to send a copy of the survey results. Ask respondents to mark a space provided on the questionnaire to indicate their interest in receiving an executive summary.

---

questions. The front cover should include the title of the survey and the official seal of the organization responsible for the project (or some other attractive design). The remaining 11 pages will contain the survey questions. When the printed pages are laid flat, before they are folded and two staples are put in place in the spine, the bottom sheet will have the cover page and page 11 on the back side and pages 1 and 10 on the front. The middle sheet will have pages 2 and 9 on the back and pages 3 and 8 on the front. The top sheet will have pages 4 and 7 on the back and pages 5 and 6 on the front. When the pages are folded, the booklet's pages will be in order. Questionnaire booklets can be made using either letter size or legal size paper.

Implementing the Mailing

Publicity about a survey in appropriate media outlets may result in an improved response rate. Press releases can explain the purpose of the survey. Internal office memos may introduce a forthcoming questionnaire for employees. If a sample is selected, not everyone in the target population will receive the questionnaire, but those who do may recall a reason to distinguish the questionnaire from junk mail if they have heard something about the survey already.

Before the envelopes are stuffed, the researcher should check to make sure that each booklet has an identification number and that this number is

The Town of Farragut
David Farragut
Mayor

May 7, 1997

Dear Ms. Jones:

The town staff is developing a budget proposal for next year and we need your help! What you think about how the council should allocate citizens' hard-earned tax dollars is *very* important to us if we are to provide the kind and quality of services that *you* want. Please take about 10 minutes from your busy schedule to tell us what you think about funding priorities and how we might be able to serve you better.

Your household is one of a small number randomly selected to participate in this project. All of your responses will remain completely confidential. No names or addresses will *ever* be connected with them. The identification number in the upper right-hand corner only helps us to confirm that you have responded, so that you won't be bothered with follow-up mailings.

Thank you for helping us with this project! Your ideas and opinions matter a great deal to us. If you would like to receive a copy of the results, just check the box on the back of the booklet and I'll see that a copy is sent to you.

Sincerely,

Joe Smith

Manager
Town of Farragut

Office of the Manager • 11320 Kingston Pike • Farragut, Tennessee 37922

Figure 4.9. Example of a Cover Letter for a First Mailing

recorded next to the name and address of the household or individual on the master list of the sampling frame. Returned, completed questionnaires should be logged on this list. The mailing package should consist of the cover letter, the questionnaire booklet, and a postage-paid self-addressed return envelope that is large enough to accommodate the booklet. Mailings should take place early in the week and all on the same day. As mentioned in Chapter 2, the use of business reply-type return envelopes can save some

The Town of Farragut
David Farragut
Mayor

May 22, 1997

Dear Ms. Jones:

About two weeks ago I wrote to you to ask for your help in establishing funding priorities for next year's town budget. Many citizens in our sample have responded so far, but we have not yet received *your* response, which is *vitally* important for the accuracy and completeness of our study.

Please take just a few minutes to answer these questions that will help us serve you better. I am enclosing another copy of the questions for your convenience. Please return them in the postage-paid envelope by May 29. I'd be happy to send you an executive summary of the results if you check the box on the last page.

Thanks so much for your help and timely action on this request. If your original response is already in the mail, you may recycle this second copy.

Sincerely,

Joe Smith

Manager
Town of Farragut

Office of the Manager • 11320 Kingston Pike • Farragut, Tennessee 37922

Figure 4.10. Example of a Cover Letter for a Second Mailing

mailing expenses, because the post office will charge the account only for the questionnaires actually returned. This also eliminates any temptation some people may have to peel off the stamp for their own use and throw away the questionnaire.

About 3 weeks after the original mailing, a second mailing should be sent to nonrespondents. In this mailing, a revised cover letter, with the new date, should courteously remind the recipients that their responses (which are vital to the study's accuracy) have not yet been received. Depending upon the response rate, a third mailing should be sent about 2 to 3 weeks after the second mailing. The cover letter in the third mailing should plead for the recipients' cooperation, underscoring the importance of their participation. If the budget permits, copies of an executive summary of the survey results may be offered to those who complete the questionnaire. If it is possible to acquire phone numbers for the procrastinators, the researcher may find that making personal requests for their help in completing the mail survey is productive. Time, effort, and attention to detail should pay off in a good return rate.

Designing the Telephone Survey

A well-designed mail questionnaire will not necessarily facilitate a good telephone interview. For telephone survey instruments many of the same guidelines apply with respect to clarity, simplicity, consistency, question order, and pretesting, but telephone surveys require attention to the needs of *three* audiences: the respondent, the interviewer, and the data entry personnel.

In a telephone interview, all communication with respondents is verbal and therefore, clarity is paramount. The respondent does not read a cover letter, examine the questions, and then decide whether or not to respond. Consequently, the vertical flow of questions and the visual attractiveness of the instrument are not important. However, the nature of the social interaction between the caller and the respondent is critical. Everything the caller does should help to establish a good rapport and a clear understanding of the questions.

The interviewer must explain clearly the purpose of the survey and indicate whether the survey is confidential or anonymous in nature. *Anonymous* responses have no identifying name or identification number; the identity of the subject is unknown even to the researcher. An assurance of *confidentiality,* in contrast, means that "the researcher agrees to limit access by others to data that can be linked to the participant" (Kimmel, 1988, p. 86). A confidential rather than anonymous interview enables the researcher to contact the same people in the future or to confirm that the interview actually took place, as a control on cheating by interviewers (Weisberg et al.,

1989). For these reasons, some researchers prefer to guarantee confidentiality rather than anonymity of responses. The case number permits the researcher to identify the respondent, but the respondent's name, affiliation, or any other identifying information is *never* linked publicly with his or her responses. The researcher must strictly limit access to the secret file that lists names and case numbers for purposes of follow-up contacts.

The dependence on oral communication in telephone interviews requires that they include less complex questions with fewer response categories than can be used in mail surveys. They should also make use of screen or branching questions to reduce the memory burden for respondents. Liberal use of transition statements and clear instructions are essential to communicate what is expected of respondents. Interviewers should read the questions at a moderate pace to give respondents time to think. It has been found that interviewers who have the lowest refusal rates are those who vary their voice pitch when reading questions (Rubenstein, 1995). Respondents find this mode of speaking more persuasive and credible than delivery of questions in a monotone or in a constant high-pitched voice. The interviewer's voice should be a little above normal volume and nonhesitant. *Key-word* summaries of response choices build in redundancy that helps respondents to understand the questions.

Telephone interviewers require questionnaires that are presented in a clear, easy-to-follow format for all questions. Pretesting of the questions is useful for detecting possible tongue twisters that can impede a listener's comprehension and test the caller's patience. The instructions in the instrument should supplement the training regime and help the caller to make smooth transitions between items. Regular placement of questions and response choices on the page helps to reduce interviewer error in marking responses.

The physical design of a telephone interview should be centered on the caller's needs. For this reason, questions should not be continued on separate pages, nor should too many questions be placed on a single page. The sheets must be easy to mark, and adequate space should be provided for interviewers to record open-ended responses.

The ability of the caller to establish credibility and rapport with potential respondents will determine the success of these social interactions. Callers must sound friendly, polite, and sincere. Patience, professionalism, empathy, and assertiveness are all desirable traits in a telephone interviewer.

Callers should read all questions precisely as they are written, without variations in wording or phrasing. Callers must also avoid any intonation that may implicitly suggest preferred responses. A telephone interview is not an occasion for "educating" respondents about desired behaviors or opinions preferred by the caller. The interviewer may at times, however, need to clarify questions that have been misunderstood, for example, "From your response, I think you must have misunderstood what we meant by a capital crime. We did not mean to refer to the corruption in the state house, but whether legislators should expand the types of crimes subject to the death penalty."

Telephone interviewing requires patience and endurance. Fatigue is a factor that should be considered. A clear, consistent coding scheme (discussed in the next chapter) will help to alleviate the strain somewhat. Generally, callers who complete four 10-minute interviews per hour have good productivity. Those who consistently contact fewer than half of the numbers on a call sheet may need additional training.

THE INTRODUCTORY SPIEL

The key to success for most telephone interviews is the introduction, which should be designed to appeal to a particular target population. The primary objectives of the introductory spiel are to persuade respondents to participate, to legitimate the survey, to build trust that the responses will remain confidential, to explain why certain information is needed, and to suggest the benefits of participation.

No single introduction is perfect for every survey, but most introductions should include the following elements:

- A greeting and the caller's complete name and affiliation
- Brief information about the purpose of the call
- A description of the selection procedure and the strict confidentiality of responses
- Information about the approximate length of the interview
- A request for permission to begin, or a request to set up an appointment to conduct an interview with the desired respondent in the household

Good callers are sensitive to potential refusals and will try in a polite way to persuade recalcitrant contacts. In an effort to salvage an interview, a caller may say something such as, "I realize that I may have called at an inconvenient time; may I call back at another time that's better for you?" or "Your opinions are really important for our study, and we want to make this as easy for you as possible. Would you prefer that I call back at a more convenient time?" If the response to such a suggestion is affirmative, the caller can then establish the time when he or she should call back. Once agreement is obtained, the caller should explain the voluntary nature of the

An introductory spiel:

Hello, my name is Grant Neely, and I'm calling for the University of Tennessee Social Science

Research Institute. We're interviewing citizens of Farragut to determine what they think about

crime in the city and what actions city officials should take to prevent or reduce various criminal

activities. Your phone number, [555-5555], was selected at random from a list of all city residents.

Is this number correct? [IF CORRECT, CONTINUE. IF NOT, POLITELY TERMINATE.]

The questions I need to ask will only take about 7 minutes to complete, and your responses will be

completely confidential, okay?

Examples of alternative screen and selection criteria:

A screen question: First, do you reside within the corporate limits of Farragut?

        [IF NO, POLITELY TERMINATE.]

Example of respondent selection criteria: Are you 18 years or older?

        [IF NO, ASK TO SPEAK WITH A PERSON IN THE HOUSEHOLD WHO IS 18 OR

        OLDER.]

Example of the last birthday selection method: To make sure our results accurately reflect the

    opinions of all city residents, I need to speak with the person in your household over 18 who

    had the most recent birthday. Are you that person?

        [IF YES, BEGIN QUESTIONS. IF NO, ASK TO SPEAK TO THAT PERSON OR

        SCHEDULE A TIME TO CALL BACK WHEN THAT INDIVIDUAL WILL BE

        AVAILABLE AND REPEAT SPIEL THEN.]

Figure 4.11. Basic Format for an Introductory Spiel and Alternative Selection
Criteria

interview with a statement such as, "Should we come to a question that you
choose not to answer, just let me know and we will move on to the next
one." Figure 4.11 shows a hypothetical introduction to a telephone interview and alternative selection criteria.

QUESTION WORDING AND
ORDER FOR TELEPHONE SURVEYS

It is essential that the researcher take special care in crafting questions
for telephone surveys because a misunderstanding of just one or two words
will affect the validity of responses. The first few questions are especially

Example of question that includes a key-word summary:

1. First, I need to ask whether you think certain crimes are a problem or not in your

   neighborhood. How about VANDALISM? Do you think it is "not a problem," "a minor problem,"

   or "a major problem" in your neighborhood?

   How about AUTO THEFTS? Do you think they are not a problem, a minor problem, or a major

   problem in your neighborhood? How about HOME BURGLARIES?

Matrix question format:

Crime	Not a Problem	Minor Problem	Major Problem	DK/NS
VANDALISM	1	2	3	4
AUTO THEFTS	1	2	3	4
HOME BURGLARIES	1	2	3	4

2. The city council is considering a proposal to establish a municipal police force. Would you

   support or oppose the idea of establishing a city police force for Farragut?

   1   NO   [Go to 3.]

   2   YES   [Go to 2a.]

   3   NOT SURE/ DON'T KNOW   [Go to 3.]

   2a. To pay for the annual cost of establishing a city police force, would you oppose or

       support the establishment of a city property tax with a rate of $1.50 per $100 of

       assessed value?

       1   STRONGLY OPPOSE

       2   OPPOSE

       3   NEITHER OPPOSE NOR FAVOR

       4   FAVOR

       5   STRONGLY FAVOR

Figure 4.11. Continued

important, because these are the "hooks" that help to convince the respondent that the survey is important and pertains to an interesting subject. If
these questions flow easily from the introduction, a sense of order is
projected that can be maintained throughout the interview.

Both Dillman (1978) and Frey (1989) recommend using a simple closed-
ended question to lead off, followed by an open-ended item. Whatever

question type is chosen, there should be no ambiguity about its connection to the purpose of study. Questions in a telephone interview should abide by the normal rules of conversation, which means the researcher should strive for a balance between simplicity and specificity. Rapport is disrupted if questions are too complex. A question should be explained to a respondent if the need or request arises. This strategy suggests a more active role for the interviewer than traditionally has been the case, and it underscores the need for the survey manager to brief callers thoroughly on the "purpose of questions and what is being measured" (Bradburn & Sudman, 1991, p. 36).

Frey (1989), Dillman (1978), and Payne (1951) suggest additional principles researchers should apply when deciding on question wording and order:

- Group questions by topic and use transitional statements to introduce survey topics.
- Think about how the order of questions might affect later responses.
- Vary the question structure where possible to hold respondents' interest and to reduce fatigue, which usually occurs after about four questions of a similar type.
- Make sure that all response categories are balanced and mutually exclusive.
- Avoid breaking a question between pages and use sufficient spacing between items to enhance readability of the instrument for the callers.
- Use lowercase type for questions and uppercase type for answers and interviewer instructions.
- Write clear instructions for all screen or filter questions.
- Pretest the questionnaire on a small sample of the target population.

Pretesting the Questions and the Instrument

Pretesting questions is one of those hallowed practices of survey research honored too often in the breach (Converse & Presser, 1986). This is unfortunate, because pretesting is a critical quality-control device. It permits the researcher to discover just how well the survey instrument works. This is the opportunity to identify and correct problems with question wording, questionnaire structure, or administration. The time spent planning and pretesting the instrument is directly related to the quality of results.

The researcher should resist the temptation to implement the questionnaire immediately after consensus is reached among the staff and survey sponsors about what to ask and how to ask it. Such consensus should not be considered to be chiseled in stone. Questions that make perfect sense to everyone in the office may confuse respondents and evoke unexpected answers. In this event, the validity of such items is doubtful. Questions examined individually may appear satisfactory, but they might be misplaced in the questionnaire, disrupt the flow of an interview, or create priming effects and position bias. Moreover, questions that *read* well may *sound* confusing to a respondent during a telephone or personal interview. Confusion can be created by homophones such as *cash* and *cache, no* and *know,* and *profit* and *prophet.* Also, interviewers might find some words difficult to pronounce.

What should researchers look for in a pretest? Fowler (1993) suggests that supervisors listen to telephone interviews with 20 to 50 respondents drawn randomly from the target population. *Each* question should be evaluated on three criteria:

- How easily the caller can read the question as worded
- Whether respondents understand the question consistently
- Whether respondents answer the question accurately with the response choices provided

Problems occur when interviewers do not read each question as worded, respondents regularly ask for clarification of questions' meanings, or respondents give inadequate or inappropriate answers (Fowler, 1993). A simple "problem-no problem" rating can be used to evaluate questions. If problems occur for given questions in more than 15% of the interviews, "those questions are either highly likely to produce distorted data or distinctively susceptible to interviewer effects" (Fowler, 1993, p. 102). Interviewer debriefings and the observed difficulties should indicate to the researcher which questions need to be revised, relocated, or deleted.

Pretesting self-administered questionnaires is even more challenging than pretesting telephone questionnaires. Instruments that will be self-administered merit especially close scrutiny during pretesting because they offer no opportunity to clarify questions' meanings or to probe for more complete responses. A two-stage procedure is recommended. First, a focus group session provides an excellent opportunity for the researcher to observe and record the time it takes individuals to complete the questionnaire. Participants can be asked about the clarity of instructions and the meanings of questions. The researcher can then correct any problems in the questionnaire that lead to difficulties in understanding or answering items prior to the second stage of the pretest. In the second stage, the researcher mails questionnaires to 20 to 50 persons in the target population. This exercise can give the investigator some idea about what type of return rate to expect and which questions are skipped or misinterpreted.

Converse and Presser (1986) offer additional guidelines for evaluating specific questions and the instrument as a whole. Tests for specific questions include variation, meaning, task difficulty, and respondents' interest and attention. Tests for the questionnaire as a whole include examination of question flow, question order, skip patterns, and completion time.

By pretesting the instrument, the researcher can ascertain whether a question measures an acceptable level of *variation* in the target population (Converse & Presser, 1986). There may be too many or too few response choices, depending on the distribution of results. If hardly anyone selects the extreme categories of a response set, then perhaps the number of choices in the scale can be collapsed. If individuals fill in or state preferences that are not offered, the choices can be expanded. If everyone selects the same response, then the question may be retained, dropped, or structured differently.

One of the most important purposes of a pretest is to clear up any confusion about the *meaning* of a question. People expect survey questions to be reasonable. They tend to "transform obscure questions into ones that seem sensible from their standpoint as they strain for meaning" (Converse & Presser, 1986, p. 57). This makes it difficult for researchers to detect misinterpretations, but one way to do so is to compare responses on similar items, as described above in the section on acquiescence response bias. For example, a seemingly innocuous question such as, "How many times during 1996 did you visit the county courthouse?" may create problems. A suspicious person might interpret this to be a subtle inquiry about his or her criminal activity if he or she thinks only about the court cases that are heard at the courthouse. Other reasonable people might think of a "visit" as a guided tour that tourists take. If both types of respondents answer "never" to this question, yet also indicate in response to another question that they paid their vehicle registration fees in person at the courthouse, there is an obvious misinterpretation. Focus groups can detect these types of problems.

Task difficulty refers to questions that tax a respondent's memory or present an unfamiliar context. Memory distortion, or "telescoping," is common when persons try to answer questions concerning events that took place over an extended period. Questions should incorporate measurement units that are familiar. Few people think about their income in "net terms" or about the economic status of the households in which they were raised in terms of a choice between classes such as "poverty," "near poverty," "working class," "middle class," or "affluent." Clear, mutually exclusive categories should be employed with the use of labels that most people understand.

No doubt stimulating questions help to hold a *respondent's interest and attention,* but the fact is that most of the subjects in a typical survey are hardly likely to increase anyone's respiration rate. Short questionnaires with varied question types can help to reduce boredom and monotony. The pretest should help the researcher identify those questions and portions of the instrument where respondent interest or attention flags. Focus group participants can rate how interesting they find the instrument as a whole.

A sensible, logical *question flow* includes brief transitions to introduce batteries of interesting questions on different topics or issues. Following the guide for question order discussed above, the respondents in the pretest can be asked how they view the connection between the leadoff questions and the stated purposes of the questionnaire. The pretest also gives the researcher the chance to correct problems with *skip patterns* dictated by interviewer instructions, which direct interviewers to vault over or to include certain sections, depending on previous responses.

The actual *time* required to complete the instrument can be observed in the pretest. Researchers should never rely on how long it takes them to complete an instrument in simulations. In practice, it always takes longer for members of the target population to complete a questionnaire.

Training Callers and
Implementing the Telephone Survey

Publicizing a forthcoming telephone survey in a community helps to reduce the number of hang-ups and refusals. Press releases to local newspapers and radio stations can stimulate stories that describe the purpose of the survey and who is conducting it. The precise days when calls are scheduled to begin should not be publicized, however, in order to avoid the possibility of sabotage by certain groups or individuals in a community.

The time required to complete a telephone survey project depends on the size of the sample, the number of callers and phones available, the length of the questionnaire, the skill and experience of the callers, and the target population. Calls should be placed at times when it is most likely respondents can be reached. Typically, fewer than half of all interviews are completed successfully on the first dialing. Interviews should be scheduled for the days and times when the highest proportion of calls are completed on the first dialing. Usually, these times are after 5:30 p.m. on weekdays, 10:30 a.m. to 5:00 p.m. on Saturdays, and 1:00 p.m. to 8:00 p.m. on Sundays. Researchers should avoid scheduling interview calls on holidays, football Saturdays, and other special-event days unique to certain jurisdictions. Calls made only during normal business hours tend to reach mostly retirees, homemakers, and college students. The number of interviews that can be completed per hour will depend upon time lost in dealing with busy signals, answering machines, nonresidential numbers, refusals, and making appointments for callbacks. The more screen questions included in the instrument, the fewer the number of completions possible per caller per hour.

An "in-house" telephone survey can employ volunteers (either public employees or others) as long as they are reliable individuals who have a pleasant demeanor and clear diction. Telephone interviewing is demanding work, and attracting and retaining good callers usually requires payment of fair compensation—more than just minimum wage. It is imperative that the researcher train all callers thoroughly. Each should understand the purpose of the interview, the meanings of questions, how to remain nondirective and unbiased in reading questions, how to handle all screen and branching questions, and how to record respondents' answers on the interview sheets (or how the software does that if a computer-assisted telephone interviewing system is used). Callers also must understand the protocol for making callbacks and for recording the disposition of attempted contacts on the call sheets. In addition, they should know how to respond to the most probable types of respondents' questions. Typically, these include questions such as the following: Who is paying for the survey? Who is in charge of the survey? How did you get my number or name? How can I be sure that my answers will be confidential? Are you going to ask me for money? Can I get a copy of the results?

A supervisor should monitor interviewer performance and be available to answer any peculiar questions that arise. Permitting callers to conduct interviews from their home telephones is not recommended. The supervisor is responsible for distributing the call sheets to each interviewer for each shift (giving workers fewer call sheets than they can complete during a shift is one way to impart a sense of progress). The supervisor should track the disposition and progress of the calls and inspect the accuracy and readability of the completed questionnaires. Prompt, thorough oversight of telephone interviews helps to reduce errors and avert potential disasters.

The callers should sign their call sheets so that the supervisor can review each person's work and assess individual callers' productivity.

Training telephone interviewers is similar to training interviewers who conduct face-to-face interviews. All questions must be asked in the proper sequence and precisely as written. Interviewers should speak slowly, clearly, and with well-modulated voices (Dillman, 1978; Singleton et al., 1993). A good training strategy is for the researcher to explain the project's purpose, process, and embedded survey instructions and to conduct *mock interview sessions* in which supervisors assume the roles of caller and respondent. Then, each of the callers practices the role of interviewer, with supervisors playing the role of respondent. This is an opportunity for the callers to experience some of the typical curves that will be thrown at them during actual calls, such as refusals, misunderstandings of questions, abusive attitudes, and unclear or incoherent responses to open-ended questions. An investment of a few hours in this type of training will yield large dividends in later consistency and accuracy. Callers will have more confidence and enthusiasm, make fewer mistakes, and appreciate how vital it is to obtain cooperation from those contacted.

Summary

Composing good questions is the key to the achievement of survey success and requires the researcher to balance specificity and simplicity to obtain valid and reliable responses. Clear, succinct, and relatively brief questions are usually preferred. The use of open-ended or closed-ended question formats depends on what information the researcher needs to know and whether exhaustive and mutually exclusive response categories can be devised. The investigator should recognize problems with double-barreled questions, false assumptions about respondents' knowledge, double negatives, loaded phrases or terms, unclear criteria, unbalanced response options, and possible sources of social desirability bias. Questions on sensitive topics require special craftsmanship and should be asked near the end of the survey. Valid opinion measures for complex concepts can be achieved through the construction of indexes. A logically organized and attractively designed instrument is a fundamental courtesy and signifies respect for the respondent's time.

The order and presentation of questions will affect the response rate and the operational validity of the questions. For a mail survey, presentation of questions in an interesting, visually pleasing way should be complemented by a cover letter that persuades potential respondents to complete the instrument. For telephone and personal interviews, training the survey personnel and supervising their work is essential for the realization of the advantages of these methods of citizen contact. Callers who establish rapport and communicate questions clearly, consistently, and accurately are more productive and make fewer errors on instruments designed especially for their use.

5

Coding and Data Entry

User-friendly statistical software programs and affordable personal computers with gigabits of memory and ultrafast microprocessors now enable just about any public organization to create and analyze huge data sets. Public administrators can use word processing, computer graphics, and laser printers to prepare polished reports and slide shows that rival the products that come from professional polling firms. In the downsized public agency of the 1990s, public administrators have additional responsibilities that attend the liberation from expensive mainframes, computer programmers, and professional drafters.

The technological advances that have been made in computer software and hardware simplify the mechanics of questionnaire design, data coding, and data analysis. Nonetheless, the old saw "Garbage in, garbage out" still applies. Researchers are responsible for designing logical coding systems that will enable them to analyze survey data in the ways desired. The better one can visualize how survey data will be analyzed and how they will serve specific information objectives, the more likely it is one can avoid problems with coding, processing, and analysis. Researchers also need to know how to detect and correct data entry errors. This chapter reviews the procedures for devising a logical coding scheme, preparing a codebook, and detecting and correcting data entry errors. The merits of computer-assisted telephone interviewing are also discussed; these will interest readers whose agencies conduct surveys on a regular basis.

The Coding Process

Coding is the process of assigning a unique variable name to each question and numbers to the answers (or nonresponses), so that electronic data analyses are possible. The coding of questions and responses should be completed *before* the instrument is implemented. This practice serves two purposes: First, a precoded instrument saves many hours that might be spent transferring data to a code sheet prior to data entry in a computer file; second, it ensures that the kind of information needed about the responses can be generated by the statistical software. Coding is a task largely invisible to consumers of the results, but it is nonetheless a very important part of planning the survey project.

Coding closed-ended questions with ordered responses is straightforward, because the respondent usually is asked to select only one answer choice. The response code is simply the number designated for that choice. Suppose, however, that a closed-ended question with unordered response choices requests respondents to "circle all that apply" in a list of services used during a particular time. Perhaps the investigator wants to know the frequency with which people use, visit, or attend various services, sites, or functions. How are multiple answers to one question coded? One solution is to designate each response as a variable and assign a code of 1 if the respondent selects a response and 0 if it is not selected. Later tabulation of the 0s and 1s for all of the cases measures the frequency of service use by respondents.

Researchers should take the following steps in carrying out coding and data entry:

1. Select a statistical software program to use in creating the data file and analyzing the data, then review the specific conventions the program requires for file formats, variable names, and missing data.
2. Devise a consistent coding scheme that is recorded in a codebook.
3. Enter the record of responses for each case into the data file.
4. Clean the data file to correct any data entry errors prior to analysis.

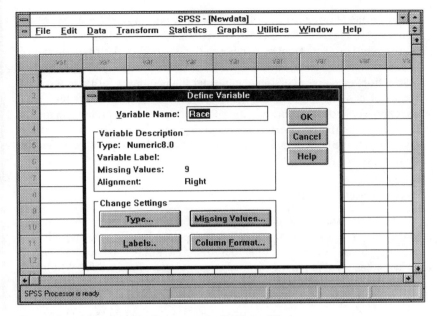

Figure 5.1. Variable Definition Screen in SPSS for Windows

SELECTING THE STATISTICAL SOFTWARE

There are many statistical software programs available for personal computers. SPSS for Windows®, Excel®, SYSTAT for Windows®, and WINSAS® are all user-friendly packages that virtually any organization with a Windows® environment can employ to create and analyze data files. These programs have straightforward menus and conventions for creating data files. The screens typically resemble spreadsheets, with rows for case records and columns for the variables. All of the data for a particular case constitute a *record*. In SPSS for Windows, variables are defined and labels are created for the different code values for the possible responses to each variable. The record for each case constitutes a separate row in the spreadsheet format. The code that matches a case's response for a variable is entered in the cell under the column designated for that variable.

The survey researcher creates the data file "template" that defines all of the variables and assigns value labels to the responses or nonresponses. This practice ensures that the data file reflects the project's coding scheme. Figure 5.1 illustrates the screen in SPSS for Windows that defines variables. It shows the variable Race entered in the variable name box. Mouse clicks on the "buttons" for variable label and missing values define those items, respectively. After this information is entered, a click on the "OK" button places this particular variable in the heading of the first column of the spreadsheet. Clearly, this is not rocket science. After a brief period of instruction, data entry personnel can enter the responses for their assigned stacks of cases in the data file template created by the researcher. After checking for and correcting any data entry errors, the researcher can merge all the data entry workers' files to create one large data file prior to analysis. The SPSS help facility has clear, step-by-step instructions for merging files.

THE CODING SCHEME

The coding scheme should follow the operationalization of the variables in the survey and should be consistent, logical, and easy to interpret. Every coding scheme assigns a unique identification number to each case. Each variable has a unique name (limited to eight letters in SPSS for Windows) and codes for each of the possible responses to it. Missing values designate the questions that are unanswered by respondents or skipped by the interviewer because they are inapplicable. Some researchers assign a code to respondents who refuse to answer a question, to differentiate them from those who do not answer for other reasons. Beyond these considerations, the question structure and the information needed by the researcher govern the coding scheme. What results is a data file in which each cell in the spreadsheet has a value in it for each case in the survey.

A consistent and logical coding scheme helps to reduce data entry errors and facilitates interpretation of the output from later statistical routines. Identical response sets should have the same coding scheme. A simple "no, yes, and don't know" set, for instance, should be coded 0, 1, 2 or 1, 2, 3 consistently. When possible, the researcher should use the same code number for a "don't know/not sure" response. Likewise, the missing value code should be the same across questions. The convention is to use a 9 or 99 for the missing value code. Technically, any code number can be assigned for a missing value, as long as it is not used or capable of being selected by a respondent to signify something other than a missing value. Forethought will help to avert later data entry and analysis problems. An open-ended question, for instance, may inquire about household size, the last grade of formal education completed, or the frequency of some behavior. In these cases, it is better to use 99 or 999 instead of simply 9, because the latter could be a respondent's answer for one of these questions. Researchers should avoid using 0 for the missing value code, as this may be a legitimate value for some responses.

A logical coding scheme typically assigns higher values for responses that signify more of something or a more positive orientation toward some object. In a Likert scale with five responses, a 1 designates the "strongly disagree" response and a 5 designates the "strongly agree" choice. The neutral "neither agree nor disagree" response is coded 3 consistently. Occasionally, even unordered response choices from a list of behaviors or opinions have an implicit hierarchy. The coding scheme should follow this logic. An exception to this convention is when respondents rank items in a list. The prevailing cultural approach to this task suggests that the respondents place a 1 by the item with a first-place ranking, a 2 by the second most important item, and so on. The researcher calculates the mean ranking of items and interprets the one with the lowest mean as the most important or highest ranked.

CODING OPEN-ENDED QUESTIONS

For partially closed-ended and completely open-ended questions, the researcher assigns numbers to represent categories made up of substantively similar responses. The exception is an open-ended question that asks the respondent to enter some type of interval-level data. For example, the numbers given in response to questions about the number of years an individual has held a position or the number of times a citizen has called city hall to report a road hazard during a particular year are simply entered in the appropriate cells in the data file. Codes are unnecessary for interval-level responses. For other types of open-ended questions, coding is required if enough responses are received to make the effort worthwhile.

The primary objective in coding open-ended questions is to devise mutually exclusive and exhaustive categories comprising a sufficient number of cases to permit meaningful analysis and comparison. When respondents answer a question in their own words, it is exceedingly difficult to anticipate what categories may emerge. For this reason, open-ended responses are grouped and coded *after* they are received. One or two persons should independently group answers to enhance coding reliability. Their efforts should be compared and a consensus reached with peers on the categories and the cases that constitute them. This consensus categorization should preserve meaningful distinctions but should not be so fine that there are only a few cases in each category. Unless the target population is very small, categories with only a few cases defeat the purpose of the coding effort and make it difficult to analyze the results. Imagine how arduous it would be to try to generalize about popular opinions for an item with 35 categories and only a handful of cases in each.

The coding process for responses to open-ended questions is inherently subjective, but usually the purpose of the survey suggests a basic rationale for classifying cases into distinct, parsimonious, and analytically meaningful groups. Inevitably, there are some cases that do not fit well into any category. These cases should receive a code for an "other" category. For mail surveys, coding open-ended responses is easier if they are recorded by case number (and variable name) as they are received. Categories usually emerge as returns arrive.

THE CODEBOOK

The codebook should list each question, its variable name, the possible response choices, the values for the responses, and the code for missing data or refusals. The codebook is the definitive statement about the rules established for the coding scheme. It is the primary guide for creating the data file template in the statistical software. Data entry is easier if the codebook and data file list the variables and codes in the order they appear in the questionnaire. Figure 5.2 illustrates a portion of a codebook for a telephone survey of city residents.

Item Q3a in the figure is an open-ended question asked only of those respondents who answered yes to Question Q3. The category codes were devised after all the responses were studied. Question Q7 illustrates an unordered response set in which the respondents indicate whether they would take each of the listed materials at least monthly to a drop-off center. Each material is coded as a distinct variable.

Data Entry

There are three basic methods for data entry:

1. Transfer of responses to code sheets and then to the data file
2. Direct entry from the questionnaires into the data file
3. Automated entry with computer-assisted telephone interview software

The last two of these methods are the most frequently used in contemporary survey research.

Question	Variable Name	Value Codes for Responses
ID Number	ID	001-624
Q1. Is curbside pick-up available at your residence?	Curbpick	1 = No 2 = Yes 9 = Missing
Q2. Does your household currently participate in the city's curbside recycling program?	Curbsidp	1 = No 2 = Yes 9 = Missing
Q3. Does your household currently participate in the city's drop-off recycling program?	Dropoffp	1 = No 2 = Yes 9 = Missing
Q3a. What suggestions do you have for improving the drop-off recycling facility that you use?	Doimprov	1 = Increase collection freq. 2 = Clean up spilled materials 3 = Add more bins 4 = Mark bins more clearly 5 = Aluminum bins need larger openings 6 = Spray for bees/wasps 7 = Other 8 = Not applicable 9 = Missing
Q4. Right now, only some neighborhoods get their recyclables picked up at the curb as part of a pilot program. Would you favor or oppose expanding curbside recycling to all city households?	Expncurb	1 = Oppose 2 = Favor 3 = Not Sure/Don't Know 9 = Missing

•
•
•

Q7. Would you be willing to take any of the following materials at least monthly to a drop-off center?	(Newspaper)	NEWS	0 = No, 1 = Yes, 9 = Missing
	(Plastic bottles)	PLASTIC	0 = No, 1 = Yes, 9 = Missing
	(Aluminum cans)	ALUM	0 = No, 1 = Yes, 9 = Missing
	(Glass bottles/jars)	GLASS	0 = No, 1 = Yes, 9 = Missing

Figure 5.2. Excerpts From a Codebook for a Telephone Survey on Household Recycling Behaviors

If for some reason the codes for the responses are not printed on the instrument itself, as might be the case for a specialized interview with several open-ended questions, it is easier to transfer the coded responses to a code sheet before entering the data into the data file on the computer. Old FORTRAN forms serve this purpose well. This two-step process is time-consuming and increases the risk of transcription errors, but it is easier to enter data from a few code sheets than from scores of unwieldy, multipage questionnaires filled with handwritten responses.

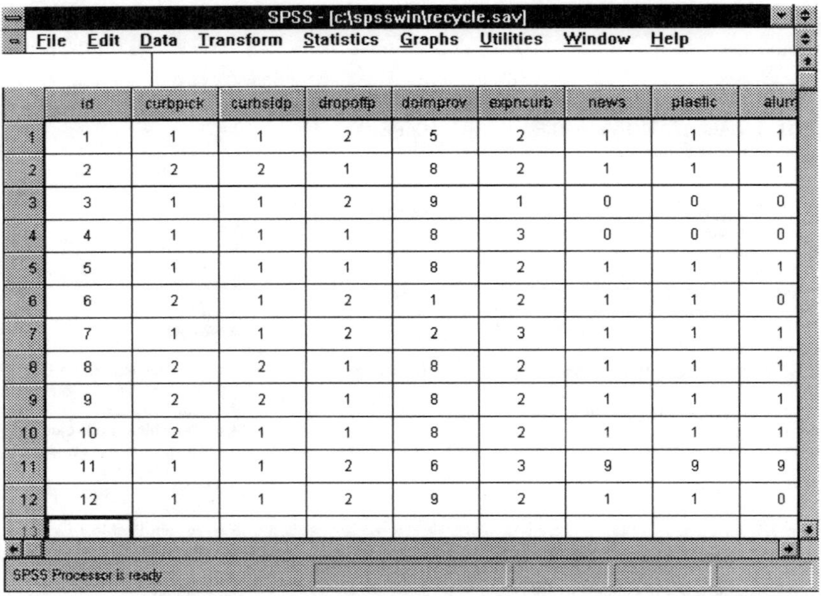

	id	curbpick	curbsidp	dropoffp	doimprov	expncurb	news	plastic	alum
1	1	1	1	2	5	2	1	1	1
2	2	2	2	1	8	2	1	1	1
3	3	1	1	2	9	1	0	0	0
4	4	1	1	1	8	3	0	0	0
5	5	1	1	1	8	2	1	1	1
6	6	2	1	2	1	2	1	1	0
7	7	1	1	2	2	3	1	1	1
8	8	2	2	1	8	2	1	1	1
9	9	2	2	1	8	2	1	1	1
10	10	2	1	1	8	2	1	1	1
11	11	1	1	2	6	3	9	9	9
12	12	1	1	2	9	2	1	1	0

SPSS - [c:\spsswin\recycle.sav]

File   Edit   Data   Transform   Statistics   Graphs   Utilities   Window   Help

SPSS Processor is ready

Figure 5.3. A Data File Created in SPSS for Windows

Usually, the questionnaire design incorporates printed codes next to the responses. This preferred practice enables data entry personnel to scan the questionnaires and enter the appropriate codes for the circled or checked responses directly into the data file. The investigator should note the appropriate code for open-ended questions in the left-hand margin to accelerate data entry and ensure consistency. Figure 5.3 displays a portion of a hypothetical data file that shows the records for 12 cases that correspond to the questions and variables in Figure 5.2.

COMPUTER-ASSISTED TELEPHONE INTERVIEWING

Software and hardware advances now make it possible to automate the data entry process for both telephone interviews and some personal interview projects. The procedures for devising a consistent and logical coding scheme still apply, but entry of valid response codes into the data file is accomplished by the caller (or even by a respondent, in a personal interview). For organizations that expect to conduct these types of interview projects regularly, an investment in this technology reduces project turnaround time and personnel costs. This technology eliminates the process of entering data from the stack of completed questionnaires, makes it unnecessary to reproduce questionnaires for callers, and saves money on labor costs for data entry personnel.

The software for a computer-assisted telephone interview (CATI) also can direct the computer to dial the phone number for computers equipped with modems. It displays the introductory spiel and prompts the caller with subsequent questions after valid response codes or verbatim comments are entered. When the interview is completed, the record of responses is stored in a file. This ASCII file is easily imported to a statistical software program for subsequent analysis. The interviewer sits at a computer terminal or a personal computer and wears a telephone headset, so his or her hands are free to enter responses on the keyboard. In this fashion, the interviewer guides the respondent through the interview and performs data entry simultaneously.

Various question processing programs are available in the marketplace. Each requires the investigator to write a program formatted for a specific questionnaire. A particularly user-friendly program that has versions for IBM PCs (or compatibles) and Macintosh computers is Ci3®, developed by Sawtooth Software, Inc. (1007 Church Street, Evanston, IL 60201). To use any CATI software, the investigator must invest the necessary time to become familiar with how it operates. The Sawtooth program is no exception, but it offers helpful pull-down menus, dialogue boxes, and an on-line help facility. Ci3 permits the investigator to use a word processor or text editor to type the text and instructions for the questionnaire. Some additional time is required to test and debug the program to ensure that it is free of errors prior to project implementation.

To use this software effectively, each interviewer must have access to a personal computer and a phone line. CATI programs ensure that only valid codes can be entered for responses, but the caller bears the ultimate responsibility for typing the codes that correctly correspond to a respondent's answers. Verification of entry accuracy is possible *only* if the supervisor calls back to repeat the interview, a practice few projects can afford. When a CATI program is used, callers must be well trained and thoroughly briefed on the importance of accurate data entry.

Despite these concerns, CATI has several distinct advantages:

- It results in faster project completion, lower cost, and fewer personnel requirements.
- It handles complex protocols and branching patterns and minimizes interviewer fatigue.

- It enables immediate tracking of respondents' profiles and tabulation of responses.
- It permits entry of only valid response codes.

The advent of highly portable laptop and notebook computers makes it possible for interviewers to use CATI programs in personal interview projects. Either the interviewer or the respondent may enter responses during the interview. Kiesler and Sproull (1986) report that when respondents enter their own answers in the computer, they are more likely to report socially undesirable behavior and to give longer answers to open-ended questions and less likely to choose "agree" or neutral responses in Likert scales. This method, called the *computer-assisted personal interview,* or CAPI, holds great potential for the design of new types of questions that include graphics, illustrations, and pictures related to the issues that concern public administrators and government officials. In the future, interviewers may even use compact discs and sound boards to show respondents video clips to accompany questions.

Data Cleaning

Data cleaning is the effort to verify, to the extent possible, the accuracy of data entry. The object is to detect and correct errors that sometimes accompany this tedious, repetitive task. Researchers can use several techniques to detect data entry errors. One method is to run frequency distributions for each variable with the selected statistical software. Cases that have invalid values for a variable are spotted easily with this method. Suppose a codebook, for instance, indicates that a variable may have only valid codes of 1, 2, 3, or 9 to represent no, yes, not sure, and missing, respectively. A value of 4 for this variable in the frequency distribution obviously signifies a data entry error. To determine the case(s) for which the error occurs, the investigator employs the "select cases" function in SPSS for Windows to instruct the computer to calculate the frequency distribution for the ID variable for cases that have a value of 4 on the variable in question. With the case number identified, the investigator consults the original instrument and enters the correct number in the case's record in the data file.

A somewhat more complicated method of data cleaning is consistency checking. Certain combinations of responses are logically inconsistent. Someone who does not participate in a Neighborhood Watch program should not report regular attendance at meetings of a Neighborhood Watch committee, for instance. Likewise, citizens who reside outside a municipality should not report that they vote in city elections. Consistency checks are useful when a questionnaire has several branching or screen questions. Cases that have a "not applicable" or "missing" value for an initial screen should not have a valid response for the subsequent question. By using the "select cases" command, the investigator can specify the logical statement that filters these cases. If any codes appear other than the appropriate ones for these cases, a probable data entry error exists and can be located and corrected according to the procedure described for the first data cleaning method.

If the CATI software is programmed correctly, data entry errors may occur only because the interviewer has typed in a number that does not represent the answer given by the respondent. Investigators may perform callbacks to check the accuracy of responses to selected items that appear suspicious or illogical.

Summary

The coding of responses to survey questions requires careful planning. The codebook is the "master plan" that contains all of the assigned values for the responses to all questions. This plan is essential to ensure that the coding scheme is consistent and logical. It ensures that the researcher can produce the kinds of analyses desired to fulfill the information objectives of the survey. Hardware and software for a CATI or CAPI system are affordable, and these are prudent investments if the organization conducts regular telephone or personal interviews. Prior to data analysis, it is important that the researcher detect and correct errors made during data entry, to ensure the accuracy of the survey.

6

Data Analysis With Computers

This chapter introduces the procedures for summarizing and analyzing survey findings using SPSS for Windows software and suggests guidelines for creating computer graphics to highlight important findings. The focus is on how to apply and interpret statistics appropriate for the data and objectives of a survey. Students and practitioners of public administration do not have to wear plastic pocket protectors or have proficiency in advanced calculus to analyze and present survey results properly. Excellent discussions of the logic, application, and interpretation of statistics are found in several methods texts, such as those by Babbie (1995), O'Sullivan and Rassel (1995), Meier and Brudney (1993), and Blalock (1979). The reader should consult one of these sources for more information about the methods introduced in this chapter.

Statistics are important tools for discovery. They help us to recognize and understand relationships among variables and causal connections between phenomena. It is important to understand both their potential and their limitations and to be able to distinguish between findings that are just statistically significant and those that are substantively important. With this level of statistical knowledge, it is possible to avoid the professionally embarrassing condition known as "falling victim to the numbers." This occurs when we endow statistical findings with a mystical quality of certitude, or when we fail to question the survey work of others simply because we equate the extensive use of Greek letters with analytic competence.

This chapter introduces the main considerations for selecting and interpreting statistics appropriate for many of the analytic tasks connected with summarizing survey results, describing and explaining relationships among variables, and making inferences to the larger population from a sample. Again, readers without any statistical training should consult one of the suggested methods texts for additional background on these topics.

In practice, most public administrators do not compute statistics manually. Computers do all of this work. What administrators must know is how to select the statistics appropriate for various data analysis tasks, how to get the computer to calculate them, and how to interpret and present the results correctly. The following sections suggest guidelines for using statistical software to analyze data and to construct tables and charts to highlight survey findings.

A Statistical Primer

When information is gathered from all members of a population, the characteristics of that population are called *parameters*. Parameters are the actual values of such things as a population's average income, household size, and opinion distribution on any issue or policy of interest to the investigator. *Statistics* are the estimates of population parameters obtained from a sample of members from the target population.

For any analytic task, the appropriate statistic to use depends on the answers to the following questions:

- Is the intent to describe variables or to infer from a sample to a population?
- What is the level of measurement of the variable(s)?
- How many variables are involved in the analysis?

There are two basic types of statistics. *Descriptive* statistics summarize and describe the characteristics of a variable or a relationship among variables. *Inferential* statistics use tests of statistical significance to measure the probability that an observed relationship or value in a sample corresponds to the actual target population parameter. A relationship is said to be statistically significant when there is a very small chance (usually less than 5%) that a relationship of the magnitude observed would manifest itself in the data if it did not exist in the target population. Within each of the two major categories there are several statistical measures from which analysts may choose, depending on their answers to the second and third questions above.

LEVELS OF MEASUREMENT

A variable's level of measurement is central to decisions about statistical analysis and graphic displays. The variables in a survey measure concepts at the nominal, ordinal, interval, or ratio level. The investigator must identify the level of measurement for each item in the survey.

Nominal variables consist of distinct categories. Although each category has a code number, there is nothing inherently numerical about these mutually exclusive items. Each is an exclusive class that cannot be placed on a numerical scale or a continuum. Nominal variables include such things as race, gender, religious affiliation, marital status, zip code, preferred location for a recycling collection center, and whether a respondent answers yes or no to a given question. Nominal variables cannot be ranked; an individual is either black or white, female or male, married or not. With nominal variables, the researcher counts the number of cases in each category and computes the proportion of the total cases in each category.

Ordinal variables have ordered categories. These categories indicate more or less of some attribute that is rank-ordered along some dimension. It is not possible to compute the *precise* distance between cases. Ordinal variables always have an explicit hierarchy on some dimension in the response choices. For example, a 5-point service satisfaction scale has choices that range from *very dissatisfied* (coded 1) to *very satisfied* (coded 5). By calculating the number and proportion of cases in each category, we might find that 45% are very satisfied. These respondents are more satisfied than those who are just "satisfied," but we cannot measure the exact "distance" between cases on this ordinal scale. Likewise, someone with a college degree has more formal education than someone with a high school degree, but it is not accurate to say that a college graduate is twice as well educated as the person with a high school diploma.

With *interval-level* variables, it is possible to measure the precise distance between cases. Ratio variables have a meaningful zero point, whereas interval variables do not, but because the same statistics are appropriate for both types of measurement, no further distinction is made between these two measurement levels. Age, income, distance, weight, volume, response time, and household size are examples of variables that are intrinsically numerical because they have a standard unit of measurement that allows us to calculate the precise distance between cases in a common unit of measurement. Percentage minority, crime rate, and years of residence are additional examples. Interval measures convey the most information about a variable because they allow the researcher to classify, order, and array values along a clearly delineated common scale or standard. The value of an interval-level variable corresponds to the magnitude of the phenomenon being measured. Dollars in a department's budget, agency staff size, and the number of clients served are measures that permit calculation of the precise distance between cases in their respective measurement standards.

Occasionally, it is difficult to discern the level of measurement of a variable because we think *only* about its typical unit of measurement and not how the survey question actually measures it. For example, income is intrinsically numerical, but if a question asks the respondent to indicate the range in which his or her 1997 total household income falls, the categories measure income only at the ordinal level. For some analytic purposes, ordinal measures of typically interval-level data are sufficient.

The hierarchy of interval, ordinal, and nominal data is important for selection of the correct statistic for data analysis. Interval data, the highest level, can be grouped into categories and treated as ordinal data for some analytic objectives. Ordinal data can be treated as nominal data, the lowest level of measurement. Measurement shifts in the opposite direction are generally not possible without special theoretical justification (Weisberg, Krosnick, & Bowen, 1989). The statistics appropriate for various analytic tasks follow this measurement hierarchy.

The following sections discuss statistics appropriate for the number of variables in an analysis. Univariate statistics measure something about the distribution of values on a single variable, bivariate statistics measure associations between two variables, and multivariate statistics can be used to analyze the simultaneous relationships among three or more variables. For the last two measurement cases, it is important to distinguish between dependent and independent variables.

Univariate Analysis

One of the researcher's first and most important data analysis tasks is to tabulate the survey results and describe these with measures of central tendency that indicate the typical value in a distribution of responses to a variable. Univariate analyses are often sufficient for many information objectives. How many people are satisfied with firefighters' response time? How many citizens support the sales tax proposal? What kind of complaints do people have about the county highway paving program? Will residents be willing to accept a cutback in street cleaning to hold the line on property taxes? To answer such questions, one calculates the number and percentage of cases in each response category.

A *frequency distribution* indicates the number of cases with each of the possible values on a single variable. A *percentage distribution* shows the proportion of total cases with a particular value on a variable. Tables of frequencies and percentages are an effective way to communicate response distributions for a variable.

PRESENTING SURVEY RESULTS IN TABLES

A properly constructed table that presents survey results has a brief descriptive title, indicates when the data were collected or the time period represented by the information, duplicates the question in a subtitle or provides labels for the response choices, and includes labels on the rows and columns. It is especially important that the table include the *base,* or the total number of cases used to compute proportions in percentage distributions. Tables display the result of grouping cases with similar values on a variable (or variables) and counting them. A single table may include several univariate distributions.

The level of variable measurement affects table design. Normally, nominal- and ordinal-level variables have relatively few categories and are easy to summarize in tabular form. Interval-level variables may require the creation of categories to "collapse" a long list of values into ordinal categories to display information parsimoniously in a table. Collapsing the interval-level data into ordinal categories sacrifices detail in favor of presenting the information in a manageable form. What category sizes are appropriate for collapsing data? This depends on the substantive point of the distribution. The ranges should be detailed enough to capture the important differences among cases, but not so small that the table size becomes difficult to understand or interpret.

Table 6.1 shows frequency and percentage distributions for nominal, ordinal, and interval variables. The table presents responses to a hypothetical questionnaire sent to a sample of 400 cities. It is important to include the total number of cases that make up the base for the percentages, because

TABLE 6.1 Frequency and Percentage Distributions

For a Nominal-Level Variable

Incentives Used in 1999 by U.S. Cities to Increase Citizen Participation in Recycling

"What incentives did your city employ to increase citizen participation in solid waste recycling during 1999?"

Incentive	Number	Percentage
Volume-based solid waste fees	121	41.9
Official recognition of neighborhood recycling accomplishments	92	31.8
School programs that encouraged children to recycle at home	76	26.3
Total	289	100

For an Ordinal-Level Variable

The Importance of Community Group Meetings in Recycling Program Design

"How important were meetings with community groups in making decisions about the design of the recycling program?"

Response	Frequency	Percentage
Important	245	61.7
Somewhat important	109	27.5
Not important	23	5.8
Don't know/not sure	20	5.0
Total	397	100

For an Interval-Level Variable

Tons of Waste Recycled in 1999 for a Sample of 400 U.S. Cities

"Approximately how many tons of solid waste were recycled in your city during 1999?"

Tons Recycled	Number of Cities	Percentage of Cities
Fewer than 100	103	25.75
100-200	128	32.00
201-300	66	16.50
301-400	73	18.25
More than 400	30	7.50
Total	400	100

not all respondents answer every question, as illustrated in the nominal example. From the base, the reader can compute that about 72% (289 of 400) of respondents answered this question. The interval-level example presents five ranges for the responses to this open-ended question. This collapses the interval-level data so that the reader can grasp the substantively important point that more than half of the cities recycled 200 or fewer tons in 1999.

TABLE 6.2 Levels of Measurement and Univariate Statistics

Variable's Level of Measurement	Measures of Central Tendency	Measures of Dispersion
Nominal	Mode	Proportion in modal group
Ordinal	Mode, median	Range, interquartile range
Interval or ratio	Mode, median, mean	Range, interquartile range, standard deviation, variance

MEASURES OF CENTRAL TENDENCY AND DISPERSION

Measures of central tendency are efficient ways to describe and summarize a distribution. They indicate the most typical value in a distribution and tell what the typical person thinks or what the central value is in a distribution. They simply substitute one number for many to describe a large number of responses. The mode, median, and mean are measures of central tendency, and they are often reported at the bottom of frequency and percentage distribution tables for the variables to which they apply.

The *mode* is the value for a variable that occurs most frequently. The *median* is the midpoint, or the middle number in an array of values arranged from highest to lowest (order of magnitude). If there is an even number of values, the median is the mean of the two middle values. In the array of numbers 6, 7, 7, 10, 14, 19, 33, 42, for example, the median is 12, which is the mean of 10 and 14, the two middle numbers. Half the scores are above and half are below the median. The *mean* is the arithmetic average calculated by adding the values of a distribution and dividing by the total number of scores. Because the mean is sensitive to extreme scores, the median may be a better measure of the typical case in a distribution.

A variable's level of measurement determines which central tendency statistics can be calculated. Following the measurement hierarchy, the mode describes nominal variables. Both the mode and the median are appropriate for ordinal data. The mode, median, and mean can describe interval-level data. In Table 6.1, for instance, all three measures of central tendency are appropriate for the interval-level example because the original data were collected at this level. Table 6.2 lists the measures of central tendency and dispersion appropriate for variables at the different measurement levels.

Measures of dispersion indicate whether data in a distribution are tightly clustered or widely spread out. These can help the researcher to decide which central tendency measure is best to report. The *range* and *interquar-*

tile range indicate the dispersion of values for ordinal and interval variables. The range is the highest score minus the lowest score and is sensitive to extreme cases. The interquartile range is usually preferred because it describes the middle 50% of cases and is obtained by removing the bottom and top quarters from the distribution.

For interval-level variables, dispersion measures indicate how well the mean measures central tendency. The smaller the value of the dispersion measure, the better the mean measures central tendency. For example, the mean number of tons recycled for the five cities in Group A (90, 95, 100, 105, 110) is 100 and the range is 20. For the five cities in Group B (90, 95, 100, 105, 775), the mean is 233 tons and the range is 685. The mean for the first group is certainly a more typical score, but the mean for the second group is skewed by the extreme case. For the Group B cities, the median (100) is a better indicator of central tendency than the mean. For a large number of cases, the range and interquartile range help us to decide which measure of central tendency best describes a distribution.

The *variance* is another dispersion measure that considers the distance each case is from the mean. The sum of these squared deviations from the mean divided by the number of cases is the variance. Its measurement scale is hard to interpret, so we use the square root of the variance, which is the *standard deviation*.[1] This is one of the most widely used measures of dispersion for interval-level variables because it indicates how well the mean describes the centrality of a distribution. The smaller the standard deviation value, the better the mean describes the distribution. The higher its value, the worse the mean is as a measure of central tendency.

For example, in the two groups of cities described above, the standard deviation for Group A is 7.1 ($250/5 = 50$, $\sqrt{50} = 7.1$) and for Group B it is 271 ($367,330/5 = 73,466$, $\sqrt{73,466} = 271$). These values tell us what we readily discern from the five cases in each group: The mean for Group A describes central tendency better than the mean for Group B. With a large number of cases the standard deviation eliminates the guesswork involved in a visual scan of the data. On the basis of the size of the standard deviation relative to the mean, we can tell whether the mean or median is a more descriptive measure of central tendency.

UNIVARIATE ANALYSIS WITH SPSS FOR WINDOWS

Univariate data analysis with statistical software is a straightforward "point and click" task. After opening the data file in SPSS for Windows, the investigator selects "Statistics" and chooses "Summarize" and then

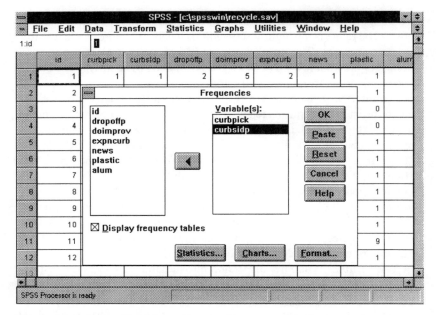

Figure 6.1. Selecting Variables to Compute Frequency Distributions and Univariate Statistics With SPSS for Windows

"Frequencies." Figure 6.1 shows the window that appears after these commands are executed for the data file "recycle.sav." This "Frequencies" window lists all of the variables in the data set on the left side of the screen. The investigator highlights the variables (with the left mouse button) for which frequency distributions are desired, and then moves these to the right side of the screen under "Variables" by clicking on the arrow between the two boxes. With the "Statistics" button at the bottom of the screen, the investigator chooses the central tendency and dispersion measures that should be computed for the variables selected.

Figure 6.1 indicates selection of the "Curbpick" and "Curbsidp" variables. The codebook page shown in Figure 5.2 shows that these are nominal variables for which the mode is the appropriate central tendency measure. Figure 6.2 is the output from the frequencies procedure when the "OK" button is selected. The data for the frequency and percentage distribution tables are found in the "Frequency" and "Valid Percent" columns of this output. The mode for both variables is 1, which represents the yes response. These simple procedures apply to any variable in a data set. One can select

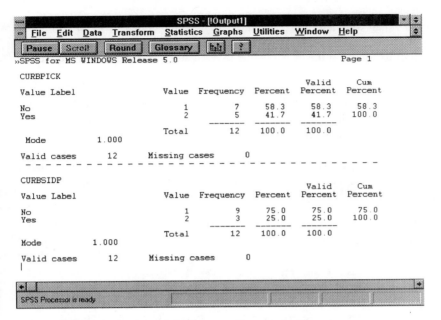

Figure 6.2. SPSS for Windows Output From Frequencies Procedure

all central tendency and dispersion measures from the "Statistics" window, and the computer will calculate these for all of the variables for which frequencies are desired. However, the investigator reports *only* those that are appropriate for a variable's level of measurement.

Bivariate Analysis

Survey objectives often require the investigator to do more than just describe distributions of popular opinions, attitudes, and behaviors. To explain *who* thinks what and to illuminate *why* they think the way they do, investigators use bivariate and multivariate statistics. Bivariate analysis examines the possible connection between a *dependent* variable, the effect we wish to explain, and an *independent* variable, the suspected cause of change in the dependent variable. For example, is a person's neighborhood (the independent variable) related to his or her evaluation of the city's pothole repair service (the dependent variable)?

When we want to explore and explain connections between things, we engage in testing propositions (hypotheses) about independent and dependent variables. In this process, the investigator seeks to answer three basic questions:

1. If the variables are related, what is the strength and direction of the relationship?
2. If the data are from a sample, is the relationship statistically significant, and, if so, is it of substantive importance?
3. Is the relationship between the independent and dependent variables *causal* in nature? Can we say, for instance, that a government welfare program causes aid recipients to avoid employment?

It is important to remember that bivariate analyses indicate only whether two variables are related (correlated). Multivariate techniques, discussed later, help to ascertain whether a causal connection exists. The procedures and statistics for answering the first two questions depend largely on the level of measurement of the variables.

When both the independent and dependent variables are either nominal- or ordinal-level measures, we construct joint frequency distributions (cross-tabulations or cross-classification tables) and employ appropriate descriptive and inferential statistics (if the data are from a sample). When the independent variable is nominal or ordinal and the dependent is interval or ratio, we compare group means or use an analysis of variance procedure. If both the independent and dependent variables are interval-level measures, investigators frequently use correlation analysis.[2] Table 6.3 summarizes the procedures and statistics appropriate for the different measurement scenarios.

CONSTRUCTING CONTINGENCY TABLES

Who is more likely to support the bond issue for the new elementary school? Do lower-income individuals play the state lottery more often than their higher-income counterparts? Is a person's educational attainment related to his or her support for citywide curbside recycling? To answer such questions, the investigator begins by constructing a contingency table according to the following steps:

1. Place the values of the independent variable at the top of the table as column heads and the values of the dependent variable along the left side as the table's row descriptors.

TABLE 6.3 Procedures and Statistics for Bivariate Analyses

Procedure: Crosstabulation

Measures of Association		*Test of Statistical Significance*
When One or Both Variables Are Nominal		Chi-Square
Statistics	**Range of Values**	
Lambda	0 to 1	
Cramer's V	0 to 1	
When Both Variables Are Ordinal		Chi-Square
Statistics	**Range of Values**	
Gamma	−1 to +1	
Tau b (for square tables)	−1 to +1	
Tau c (for nonsquare tables)	−1 to +1	

Procedure: Comparison of Means and Analysis of Variance

When Independent Variable Is Nominal or Ordinal and the Dependent Variable Is Interval or Ratio

Statistics		**Function**
Difference of means for categories of the independent variable	Indicates direction of the relationship	*t* test
Analysis of variance or eta^2	Indicates strength of the relationship (0 to 1)	*F* test

Procedure: Correlation Analysis

When Both Variables Are Interval

Statistics	**Value**	
Pearson's product-moment correlation (r)	−1 to +1	*t* test
Coefficient of determination (r^2)	0 to 1	

2. Place the cases in the survey in the table "cells" that correspond to their values on both variables. The result is an array of the joint distribution of two variables that shows the number of cases in each cell.

3. Compute the percentage of cases in each category of the independent variable so that each category or column of the independent variable totals 100%. The total number of cases (the base) should be reported for each column and the row total.

4. Interpret the table by comparing the categories of the independent variable in terms of their percentages on the values of the dependent variable.

The Crosstab Procedure in SPSS for Windows

Creating a contingency table in SPSS for Windows is a straightforward task. The analyst sequentially selects "Statistics," "Summarize," and then "Crosstabs" from the pop-up menus. In the crosstabs window, the researcher

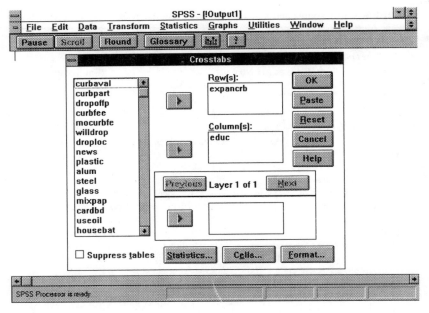

Figure 6.3. SPSS for Windows Crosstabs Procedure

selects the row or dependent variable and the column or independent variable from the variable list on the left side of the screen, as illustrated in Figure 6.3. After clicking the "Cells" button at the bottom of the screen, the analyst selects the "Column" option to display the percentages for the independent variable. Clicks on "Continue" and the "OK" buttons will then obtain output similar to that in Figure 6.4.

Figure 6.4 also illustrates output that does *not* abide by the logical order of magnitude coding scheme recommended in Chapter 5. Observe that the response choices "favor" and "oppose" are coded 1 and 2, respectively. These codes depart from the practice of assigning higher codes for responses that signify more positive orientation to an issue. So what? It makes no difference in the computation of percentages, but, as will become clear, it matters greatly in how we interpret the sign of certain descriptive statistics that tell us something about the direction of the relationship between two variables. (The code for the "not sure" response does not affect the computation of chi-square; these cases also may be excluded from a bivariate analysis.)

Table 6.4 illustrates the correct format for a contingency table based on the crosstabs output. One can edit the table directly on the output screen to

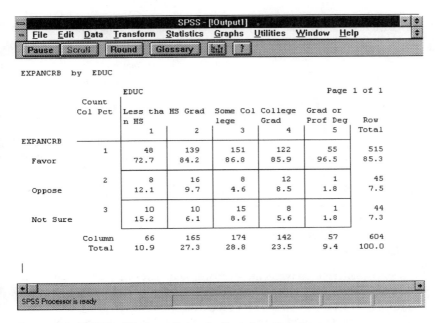

EXPANCRB by EDUC

		EDUC				Page 1 of 1	
	Count Col Pct	Less tha n HS 1	HS Grad 2	Some Col lege 3	College Grad 4	Grad or Prof Deg 5	Row Total
EXPANCRB Favor	1	48 72.7	139 84.2	151 86.8	122 85.9	55 96.5	515 85.3
Oppose	2	8 12.1	16 9.7	8 4.6	12 8.5	1 1.8	45 7.5
Not Sure	3	10 15.2	10 6.1	15 8.6	8 5.6	1 1.8	44 7.3
Column Total		66 10.9	165 27.3	174 28.8	142 23.5	57 9.4	604 100.0

Figure 6.4. SPSS for Windows Crosstabs Procedure Output

produce this format. The table follows the convention of placing the independent variable "education" at the top of the columns and the dependent variable "support for citywide curbside recycling" alongside the rows. The 604 cases are divided among the categories of education. The percentage of cases in each category of the dependent variable is computed. The number of cases in each column are arrayed at the bottom of the table.

To read this table, one compares the cases with different levels of educational attainment and their support for citywide curbside recycling. On the basis of this table, we can say that a substantial proportion of cases at each level of educational attainment favor the idea of citywide curbside recycling, but it appears that those with higher levels of formal education are even more likely to favor the idea. Is there really a relationship between the two variables? If so, what is its strength and direction? Is it statistically significant? We answer such questions by using statistics appropriate for the level of measurement of the variables. Can you identify the level of measurement for the variables in Table 6.4? You are correct if you said ordinal. First, however, let us review the statistics appropriate for nominal data, the lowest level of measurement.

TABLE 6.4 Sample Contingency Table: Popular Support in June 1999 for Citywide Curbside Recycling by Educational Attainment (in percentages)

| Opinion | Level of Educational Attainment | | | | | |
	Some High School	High School	Some College	Bachelor's Degree	Graduate/ Professional Degree	Total Number
Oppose	12.1	9.7	4.6	8.5	1.8	45
Favor	72.7	84.2	86.8	85.9	96.5	515
Not sure	15.2	6.1	8.6	5.6	1.8	44
Total percentage	100	100	100	100	100	
Number	66	165	174	142	57	604

MEASURES OF ASSOCIATION
AND STATISTICAL SIGNIFICANCE

Statistics are a convenient, standard, and efficient way to summarize data in a contingency table. They indicate whether a relationship exists, how strong it is, its direction, and its statistical significance. Only the analyst, however, can determine if an observed relationship is substantively important. Statistics are not substitutes for knowledge about a topic. Statistics measure relationships, but investigators must link these findings to a theory, purpose, or objective of import to the survey enterprise. Without the ability to interpret the substantive implications of statistical findings, the investigator cannot answer the critical "So what?" question that interests consumers of the survey.

Measures of association summarize the distribution of cases in a contingency table. The statistics for nominal data have values that range from 0 (or no relationship) to 1 (a perfect relationship). The closer the value is to 0, the weaker the relationship; the closer to 1, the stronger the association. For ordinal and interval data, the statistical values range from -1 to $+1$. The plus or minus sign that precedes the statistic indicates the direction of the relationship. For example, values of .71 and $-.71$ are equally strong, but the positive value indicates that the independent and dependent variables vary or change together in the same direction, whereas the negative value indicates that they vary or change together in opposite directions. Education and income, for instance, might have an association that measures .71, which means that as education increases, so does the level of income. Higher values on the independent variable education are associated with higher values on the dependent variable income. Conversely, household income and support for a proposed income tax (measured on a 5-point oppose-favor scale) might have an association that measures −.71, which means that as household income increases, so does opposition to the income tax. Higher values on the independent variable income are associated with lower values on the dependent variable.

What constitutes a weak, moderate, or strong statistical relationship depends on the statistic and also on what is known about the research question to which the finding pertains. Different statistics produce somewhat different values for the same relationship. This is a function of their computation and the criteria for measuring the strength of a relationship. Analysts look for comparable values on different statistics that together may suggest a weak, moderate, or strong relationship between variables. For these reasons one does not compare different statistics across relationships, or claim, for example, that a relationship with a lambda value of .07 is weaker than another relationship with a gamma of −.23.

For reasons that have to do with the computation of many statistical formulas, explanations for which are beyond the scope of this book, stronger relationships are more likely to attain statistical significance and larger sample sizes are more likely to yield statistically significant results than are small samples (Johnson & Joslyn, 1991). Accordingly, investigators must be cautious about ascribing great substantive significance to weak, statistically significant findings in large samples.

Nominal-Level Statistics

Statistics for nominal variables indicate only the strength of a relationship, not direction, because they are mutually exclusive classes and do not represent more or less of anything. Goodman and Kruskal's lambda and Cramer's V are two of the more widely used statistics to measure the strength of an association if *either* variable is nominal. Their values range from 0 to 1.

Lambda tells us whether the values of the independent variable tend to cluster around certain values of the dependent variable. It is based on the proportional reduction of error (PRE) model, which indicates how much better off we are knowing the value of the independent variable in predicting the value of the dependent variable. This means that the lambda statistic is a percentage by which we can improve a guess of a case's value on the dependent variable. For instance, if we know that 55% of respondents oppose metropolitan consolidation and 45% favor it, our guess of what *anyone* thinks about consolidation is correct more often if we guess the modal response "oppose." However, our guess about whether a person opposes or favors consolidation is likely to be correct *more often* if we know where a citizen resides *and* whether or not place of residence (city or county) relates to opinions on consolidation. The lambda value measures our improvement in prediction by knowing a case's value on the independent variable. For example, if lambda is .35 for these two variables, we improve the prediction of a case's value on the dependent variable by 35%. This value indicates a moderately strong relationship between the two nominal variables.[3] A value of .09 improves prediction by just 9% and represents a weak relationship.

Lambda is a fairly conservative statistic in that it may equal zero and ignore an apparent relationship between variables. This occurs when the mode of every value of the independent variable is in the same category of the dependent variable. It is also an asymmetric measure because its value differs depending on which variable is designated as independent. In conjunction with lambda, we use other more sensitive measures, such as Cramer's V, to measure possible relationships in a contingency table.

Cramer's V measures the strength of an association and has values that range from 0 to 1.[4] Unlike the value of lambda, its value is based on the computation of another statistic called *chi-square*. Cramer's V is a symmetric measure that has the same value regardless of which variable is independent. Typically, observed values between .20 and .40 suggest a moderate relationship, and values over .80 are encountered rarely (Poister, 1978). Nominal-level statistics *must* be used if either variable is measured at this level, but they also may be computed for ordinal-level variables because of the measurement hierarchy previously discussed.

Ordinal-Level Statistics

The most frequently used descriptive statistics for ordinal independent and dependent variables are Goodman and Kruskal's gamma, Kendall's tau b, and Kendall's tau c.[5] Each measures the strength *and* direction of a relationship. Their values range from –1 to +1. They summarize variables in a contingency table in similar but not identical ways. Each is a symmetric statistic that considers every possible pair of cases in a contingency table. The pairs are checked to see if their relative ordering on the first variable is the same as their relative ordering on the second variable (concordant) or if the ordering is reversed (discordant). Unlike gamma statistics, the tau statistics also count the number of tied pairs that have the same value on one or both variables.

Consider a crosstabulation of education and service satisfaction. Assume both variables are dichotomous (two categories), with a low category (coded 1) and a high category (coded 2). A concordant pair consists of one case with values for low education and low service satisfaction and one case with values for high education and high satisfaction. A discordant pair has one case with low education and high service satisfaction and another with high education and low service satisfaction.

Gamma represents the proportion of paired or concordant observations minus the number of discordant pairs divided by the number of concordant pairs plus the number of discordant pairs. If the numbers of both types of pairs are the same, gamma yields a value of zero. If concordant pairs are more numerous, its value is positive, and if discordant pairs are more numerous, its value is negative. The degree to which one type of pair occurs more frequently than the other determines the strength of the relationship. Gamma often produces higher values than other ordinal statistics because it ignores tied pairs in its formula. For this reason, investigators also use a tau statistic that accounts for the number of tied pairs in computing the strength of an association.

Kendall's tau b is used for square tables, where the number of rows equals the number of columns. *Kendall's tau c* is used for nonsquare tables. These measures are preferred for most ordinal-level data because they count tied pairs.

Dichotomous Variables

Dichotomous variables are a special case in decisions about the appropriate use of a statistic. When both variables have *only* two categories, such as gender, a yes or no response set, or race (measured as white or nonwhite), they can be treated as nominal, ordinal, or interval. Statistics for any of these levels are equally appropriate. The researcher must remember, however, that the sign computed by ordinal and interval statistics changes if the coding of the variable categories is switched. For example, if the independent variable is nominal and dichotomous and the dependent variable is interval, the investigator may use Pearson's product-moment correlation to measure the bivariate association. The sign of the statistic depends on how the nominal independent variable is coded.

Statistical Significance

What is the likelihood that an observed association between two variables occurs merely by chance? In other words, what is the probability an observed relationship between variables in a sample also exists in the entire population? Chi-square is the inferential test statistic that measures whether the relationship between two nominal or ordinal variables in a cross-tabulation differs significantly from a relationship that might have occurred randomly or by chance alone.[6] It is based on the idea of a *null hypothesis* that posits no relationship between the variables in the population. Chi-square indicates what the expected distribution of cases would be for a crosstabulation of two variables *if* they were not related in the population. These expected cell frequencies are compared with the actual values from the sample. The greater the differences between the expected and observed frequencies, the larger the chi-square value and the less probable it is that the observed association is due to chance alone. Smaller chi-square values indicate the absence of a relationship (statistical independence).

The expected frequencies in each cell of a table consist of the number of cases we would expect if there were *no* relationship, for instance, between education and support for citywide recycling in Table 6.4. In other words, among the different levels of education, we would *expect* 85.3% of *each* group to favor citywide recycling and 7.5% to oppose it. There would be no difference in the proportion of cases in each cell and the corresponding marginals.

The probability of obtaining a chi-square value as large as or larger than one calculated from a sample if in fact the variables are independent (not related) is computed by the Crosstabs procedure in SPSS for Windows. Remember that chi-square does not indicate the strength of a relationship. It only helps the researcher to decide if the variables are related at the probability criterion or *alpha level* set by the investigator. Most public administration researchers set the alpha level at .05 or .01, which refers to the chances of committing a Type I error.[7] Commission of a Type I error occurs when a true null hypothesis is rejected; in other words, one concludes that a statistically significant relationship exists when in fact it does not (failure to reject an untrue null hypothesis is called Type II error). Investigators do not wish to mislead anyone by claiming that a relationship exists in the population when in fact it does not, so they take only a 5% or, perhaps even more stringent, a 1% chance of committing such an error by setting the alpha levels at these probabilities.

Statistics From the SPSS for Windows Crosstab Procedure

Part of the typical crosstab procedure is to calculate statistics for contingency tables. After selection of the row (dependent) and column (inde-

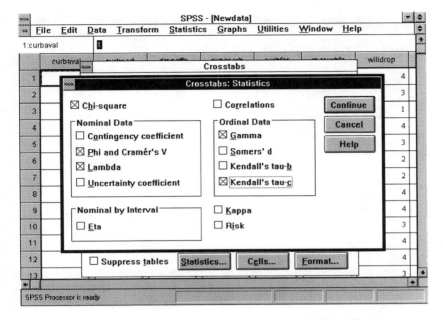

Figure 6.5. Selection of Statistics for a Crosstabulation in SPSS for Windows

pendent) variables for analysis, the investigator clicks on the "Statistics" button as shown in Figure 6.3. For the two ordinal-level variables in that example, the investigator marks the desired statistics with an X as shown in Figure 6.5 to produce the output shown in Figure 6.6.

Figure 6.5 shows the selection of chi-square for the test statistic, Cramer's V and lambda, gamma, and Kendall's tau c (for nonsquare tables). Remember that nominal measures may be computed for ordinal variables too. Clicking on "Continue" and then "OK" in the Crosstabs window will obtain statistical values such as those illustrated in Figure 6.6.

Gamma equals –.24 and tau c equals –.07. These statistics confirm that a relationship exists between educational level and support for citywide recycling. The association is rather weak considering the lower values of these two statistics. The relationship is negative *only* because the more positive opinion (favor) is coded 1 and the negative orientation (oppose) is coded 2. In this case, the negative sign means that as educational level increases, respondents are more likely to favor citywide recycling. Interpretation of the direction of a relationship is much easier if the investigator

```
                              SPSS - [!Output1]                        ▼ ⬍
  -   File   Edit   Data   Transform   Statistics   Graphs   Utilities   Window   Help      ⬍
     Pause   Scroll     Round    Glossary    📊   ?
        Chi-Square              Value          DF              Significance        ▲
     --------------------    -----------      ----           -------------
     Pearson                  19.05444          8               .01457
     Likelihood Ratio         19.85106          8               .01091
     Mantel-Haenszel test for  9.47384          1               .00208
        linear association
     Minimum Expected Frequency -   4.152
     Cells with Expected Frequency < 5 -    4 OF    15 ( 26.7%)
                                                                Approximate
        Statistic              Value        ASE1     Val/ASE0   Significance
     --------------------    ---------    --------   --------   -------------
     Phi                       .17761                            .01457 *1
     Cramer's V                .12559                            .01457 *1
     Lambda :
        symmetric             .01541       .00932    1.63661
        with EXPANCRB dependent .00000     .00000
        with EDUC     dependent .01860     .01129    1.63661
     Goodman & Kruskal Tau :
        with EXPANCRB dependent .01935     .00909               .00295 *2
        with EDUC     dependent .00595     .00291               .07288 *2
     Kendall's Tau-c          -.07334      .02442   -3.00331
     Gamma                    -.24199      .07703   -3.00331
     *1 Pearson chi-square probability
     *2 Based on chi-square approximation ;  Number of Missing Observations:   12   ▼
  ◄                                                                              ►
  SPSS Processor is ready
```

Figure 6.6. Statistics Output for SPSS for Windows Crosstabulation Procedure

abides by the logical coding scheme recommended where the more positive orientations have higher values.

Notice that lambda produces a misleading value of 0 because "favor" is the modal response for each level of education. In this circumstance, Cramer's V is more accurate because it indicates the existence of a weak association.

Is this relationship statistically significant at the .05 level? At the top of the output, we see a Pearson chi-square value of 19.05444 with 8 degrees of freedom (DF on the screen).[8] The probability of obtaining a chi-square value this large with 8 degrees of freedom is .01457, which is slightly more than a 1 in 100 chance. We conclude that a systematic relationship exists because the observed cell frequencies deviate more than what we would expect if the two variables were not related to each other. There is only about a 1.5% chance that we would be wrong about this conclusion for a table with deviations from the expected as large as the ones observed. This probability is much less than our established alpha level of .05, so the chi-square is statistically significant at the .05 level. *If* the computed probability for a chi-square were .05 or larger, the risk of being wrong would be too high, so we could not claim that a statistically significant relationship exists.

Difference of Means and Analysis of Variance

When the independent variable is nominal or ordinal and the dependent variable is interval, the investigator has two strategies for assessing a relationship's strength, direction, and statistical significance. One is to collapse the interval dependent measure into ordinal categories for analysis in a contingency table. Of course, the precision of the interval measure will be lost, because grouping cases into categories diminishes potentially important variation between cases. The second strategy is to test whether the difference between two sample means is statistically significant (which signifies a true difference between them) or to use an analysis of variance (eta^2) statistic to test the proposition (or null hypothesis) that the variables are independent. The difference of means and analysis of variance procedures have associated tests of statistical significance.

Rather than construct a contingency table, a difference of means test compares the means of the groups created with the independent variable to determine if the difference between them is statistically significant. This technique is useful for a variety of research questions. For example, does a training program for caseworkers result in a reduction of the average number of days to process a benefit claim? Is there a significant difference in the number of complaints about the parks maintained by the city versus those cared for by volunteer groups? Has the new customer service policy affected the approval rating of the planning department? Does the preventive maintenance program save the state money compared with the old policy of fixing cars in the fleet only when they break down? Assuming the elements of the samples are selected randomly, we compare the difference in the means for the groups in these examples to determine if the size of that difference for the respective "treatments" is large enough to say that they could not have occurred just by chance or sample variability.

To illustrate, assume that 100 new cars are purchased and assigned to various state departments. Half are randomly selected to receive preventive maintenance and the other half are repaired only when they break down. Detailed cost records at the end of the year indicate the mean cost for the preventive maintenance group is $625 and the mean for the other group is $700. The computed standard deviations for each group are $50 and $200, respectively. Is the mean difference sufficiently large to conclude that there is a real difference in the maintenance costs between the two groups? Is it prudent to extend the new policy to all vehicles?

The researcher sets the criterion of .05 to be 95% sure that the observed difference is not due only to chance. To reject the null hypothesis that there is no significant difference between the two means, the value of the t statistic (also called a t score) must be larger than the t value required for significance at the .05 level for the degrees of freedom in the problem. This latter value largely depends on the size of the samples, because the degrees of freedom for the t test is the sum of the two sample sizes minus 2, or $[(N_1 + N_2) - 2]$.

To compute the t value and the precise probability of the t value, we select the "Statistics," "Compare Means," and "Samples T test" options in SPSS for Windows and then select the dependent variable as the "Test variable" and the independent variable as the "Grouping variable." If the significance level of the t value is less than .05, then the difference of means is statistically significant. The investigator can say that a difference as large as the one observed would occur by chance in fewer than 5 of 100 samples of the size selected.

For the example described above, the t value equals 2.57 and the associated value in a t distribution table for 98 df is about 1.99.[9] The t value for the difference of means exceeds the critical t value for the .05 probability, so we reject the null hypothesis that there is no significant difference in maintenance costs and conclude that the preventive maintenance program does indeed represent real cost savings for the state if all new state vehicles are maintained in this way.

A more precise measure of the variance in the dependent variable explained by the independent variable is *eta-squared,* or eta². This statistic indicates the proportion of the total variation in the dependent variable accounted for by the independent variable. It is similar to a lambda statistic for a contingency table. The proportion of total explained variance will range from 0 to 1.[10] The closer eta² is to 0, the weaker the relationship; the closer it is to 1, the stronger the relationship. The statistical significance of the relationship is ascertained by a statistic called an F ratio. This value must exceed the criterion level to claim a statistically significant relationship between the two variables. The criterion level depends on the degrees of freedom and the probability of rejecting the null hypothesis (Johnson & Joslyn, 1991).

SPSS for Windows computes eta², F (the ratio of the two mean squares), and the exact probability of getting an F value at least as large as the one measured if the null hypothesis is true. If the "F Sig." value is less than .05, the relationship between the independent and dependent variables is statistically significant.

Correlation Analysis for Interval-Level Data

Statistics for interval-level variables enable the investigator to describe relationships, make inferences about the population based on the sample, claim causality, and forecast outcomes. A statistic widely used to describe the strength and direction of a relationship between two interval variables is Pearson's product-moment correlation coefficient, or r. Linear and multiple regression are other techniques that are helpful for making causal claims and predicting outcomes, but space constraints limit discussion of these methods here.[11]

Correlation (r) stems from the logic of linear regression analysis that uses the formula $y = a + b(X)$ to ascertain a straight line that is the best linear representation of the relationship between y, the dependent variable, and X, the independent variable. Assume, for example, that we select a sample of 600 cases and want to know whether a person's income (X) is related to the number of visits he or she makes to a local public health clinic (y). We could plot all of the data points on a graph (called a scattergram). A straight line that best fits the data points can be computed using the observed values of y and X to calculate the intercept (a) and the slope (b) of the line. The result is a line that attempts to minimize the vertical distances between the data points and the line. As long as the slope (b) is not zero, some relationship between X and y exists. Pearson's r indicates how close the straight line is to all of the data points. It measures the goodness of fit between the line and the data points.

The values of Pearson's r range from -1 to $+1$. The closer the value is to zero, the weaker the relationship and the farther the data points are from the regression line. Higher values indicate stronger relationships and a better fit of the line to the data points. Whereas r indicates the strength of a relationship and its sign indicates direction, the square of r (r^2) measures the proportion of variance in the dependent variable explained by the independent variable.

The squared distances from the data points to the regression line constitute unexplained variance. By subtracting this unexplained variance from 1 and dividing by the total variance, we compute a value that is analogous to eta^2 in its interpretation. The closer r^2 is to 1, the more variance in the dependent measure is explained by the independent variable. Suppose that $r = -.25$, a moderately weak relationship for income and visits to a public health clinic. Coded properly, this suggests that lower-income persons are more likely to visit the local public health clinic. The r^2 is only .0625, or 6.25%, which means that very little variance in the dependent measure is explained by a person's income. In this case, we might want to test another variable, such as age, to see if it can explain more variance and perform better in answering the research question about who is more likely to visit a public health clinic.

To calculate Pearson's r and the statistical significance of the relationship, we select the "Statistics," "Correlate," and "Bivariate" choices from the successive menus that appear in SPSS for Windows. We then select the interval or ratio variables for the correlation analysis and choose the "Display actual significance level" option. To test whether a correlation is significantly different from zero, we select the "two-tailed" test of significance option. If we have a good reason to believe that the independent variable has a particular directional effect on the independent variable, we would select the "one-tailed" option. If unsure about this, we would select the more rigorous two-tailed test. The output displays three lines of information. The top line is the r coefficient, the middle line contains the number of cases used in the computation, and the last line is the exact probability level. If the "p equals" value is less than .05, the relationship is statistically significant, meaning that we take less than a 5% chance of declaring a correlation significant when the population correlation is zero.

For instance, if $p = .0422$ for the correlation of income and clinic visits, a statistically significant relationship exists. However, this finding is unlikely to appear on the six o'clock news because we explain just over 6% of the variance. Recall that statistical significance is more likely with larger samples, so the investigator bears the responsibility of determining whether such a finding also has substantive importance in the context of the research question.

Multivariate Analysis: Controlling for Variables

Bivariate analysis indicates only whether or not two variables are related; it does not imply causality. Administrative life is multivariate. There are many factors that may effect change in a dependent measure. What causes citizens to oppose more spending on public transportation? Why do black respondents rate a particular social services agency more favorably than do white respondents? Why are teachers with more years of experience less satisfied with the quality of their working environment than are less experienced teachers? To understand more fully the apparent relationships between variables, investigators use multivariate data analysis techniques to control for the effects of other variables.

Multivariate techniques are appropriate for analytic tasks that involve three or more variables. The specific technique depends upon the level of measurement of the variables. For instance, multiple regression is used when the variables are interval measures. Logit is appropriate when the variables are nominal.[12]

This section illustrates the logic of introducing control variables in cross-tabulation analysis. The rationales for introducing control variables include the following: to eliminate rival hypotheses, to explore further the original bivariate relationship, and to determine whether or not a relationship really exists between two factors. For example, a bivariate analysis may suggest a connection between gender and being hired by a public works division. Employment data show 83 of 100 male applicants are hired, compared with 27 of 100 female applicants. Does this mean the public works division discriminates against females in hiring decisions? It appears that men have more than a threefold better chance than women of being hired. Without introducing a control variable, we might erroneously conclude that the division discriminates against female applicants.

Consider the possibility that an apparent association between two variables disappears or even reverses when a control variable is introduced. For the sake of simplicity, assume that there are two major departments in this hypothetical public service division (Engineering and Maintenance), the directors of which make the final hiring decisions. One might collect the departmental data shown in Table 6.5, which show that there is essentially *no difference* in the proportion of female and male applicants hired for jobs in each department. Men and women applicants were hired with *equal* frequency by each department. Most women applied for engineering jobs that may have been more difficult to obtain because of a special state license requirement they may not have fulfilled. Fewer women applied for the manual labor positions in the maintenance department. Whatever the reason for this differential application rate between the sexes, there is no evidence that males receive preference over females in the hiring decisions made by department directors.

This example illustrates a phenomenon known as *Simpson's paradox,* a spurious correlation between variables in a general table that disappears or reverses when the same variables are examined for the categories of a control variable.[13] It underscores the point that bivariate associations in grand tables can mislead investigators. The researcher must explore other

TABLE 6.5 Multivariate Crosstabulation

Grand Table

Gender and Hiring Decisions by the Public Service Division in 1999

Gender	Applications	Hired	Hiring Rate (%)
Males	100	83	83
Females	100	27	27

Partial Tables

Gender and Hiring Decisions in the Public Service Division, Controlling for Department

	Engineering Department			Maintenance Department		
Gender	Applications	Hired	Hiring Rate (%)	Applications	Hired	Hiring Rate (%)
Males	10	2	20	90	81	90
Females	90	18	20	10	9	90

possible explanations or causes for any apparent bivariate relationship that has policy consequences.

Elaboration modeling is one process for examining the association between two variables while controlling for the effects of a third. Contingency tables are used to examine the relationship between two variables within the categories of the control variable and to compare the results of each of the partial tables with the original bivariate table. To *control* a variable means to hold it statistically invariant or constant.

Suppose, for example, that a relationship is observed between race and support for an income tax increase. Does a person's race cause him or her to support or oppose this proposal? Perhaps a person's income relates to both race and opinion on this issue. To determine what impact, if any, income has on this relationship, we could hold its effects constant by grouping the observations into low, moderate, and high income categories. We examine the nature of the relationship between race and opinion on the income tax for cases that have the *same* value on income (low, moderate, or high). This method removes the impact of variations in income on the relationship between race and opinion.

Four possible outcomes may occur when a control variable is introduced: replication, explanation, interpretation, or specification. If the relationship between the original two variables remains basically unchanged (indicated by the measure of association) when a third variable is controlled, the term *replication* is assigned to the result. In other words, the "control" variable has no effect on the nature of the relationship between race and support for the income tax increase. The statistical measure of association for each of the "partial" tables (the categories of the control) replicates the one obtained in the original relationship. Cramer's V, for example, will be comparable for the relationship between race and opinion in each of the low, moderate, and high income categories and for the original bivariate relationship. We conclude that the original relationship is a genuine one and is not affected by the control variable.

If the original bivariate relationship disappears in the partial tables of the control variable and the control variable is antecedent to both the dependent and independent variables, the relationship is spurious. The term *explanation* describes this outcome. In this case, the measure of association in the partial tables is zero or significantly less than the value observed in the original bivariate table. This outcome means the control variable is related to both of the other two variables and accounts for *all* of their apparent covariation. In this event, we conclude that the original association is not genuine. For example, if a relationship between income and support for metropolitan consolidation disappears when we examine it within the categories of the control variable race (white and nonwhite), the original relationship is spurious because a person's race precedes income and opinion.

A spurious relationship is distinguished from a third possible outcome known as *interpretation* by the time order of the control variable. If the measures of association for both "partial" tables are close to zero, *and* the time order of the control variable *intervenes* between the independent and dependent variables, we interpret or clarify the process through which the independent variable has an effect on the dependent variable. In the example of race and opinion on the income tax, income, the control variable, is something that occurs after a person's race but usually before an opinion is formed on an issue. If the Cramer's V statistics are close to zero for the partial tables, race still has the measured effect on opinion, but we clarify the mechanics of the causal process.

Finally, if the measure of association in *one* partial table is much stronger than the one for the original bivariate association, and the other partial tables have a much smaller or near zero association, *specification* is the result. This outcome also is called *statistical interaction*. The effect of the independent variable on the dependent variable depends on the category of the control variable. This result allows us to specify the circumstances under which the independent variable causes change in the dependent variable.

To control for a variable in SPSS for Windows, we simply specify the variable in the crosstabs window in the third box under "Layer 1 of 1" (see Figure 6.3). The output produces partial tables for each of the categories of the control variable.

Creating Charts to Summarize Findings

Charts are useful for summarizing and communicating important findings of survey research. Designed correctly, they are an excellent way to "illustrate, describe, elucidate, interpret, and transmit information" (Schmid, 1983, p. 3). Public officials and citizens can comprehend opinion distributions, complex relationships, and trends more easily if they are presented through the *judicious* use of visual aids. Charts are easy to create with contemporary software, but investigators should resist the temptation to include an overabundance of illustrations in their reports. The sparing use of charts is more effective and focuses consumer attention on the most salient findings.

A good chart has the following characteristics:

- It accurately represents the data.
- It has a clear purpose (it may describe, compare, tabulate, or encourage the reader to think about particular information).
- It is attractive and easy to understand without explanatory text.
- It has a brief descriptive title and appropriate labels or legends that identify data series or pie slices.

Well-designed charts do not use overpowering fonts or bizarre, obscure patterns. The font sizes are large enough to enable viewers to discern the information from whatever distance they are expected to see it. The simpler the chart, the easier it is for the audience to grasp its purpose in the time available to view it. The order of the information presented in a chart should follow common sense and should enable the viewer to detect readily the differences, changes, or trends the investigator wishes to communicate. The measurement scale should be clearly understandable and should represent the data accurately. For line and bar charts, the vertical or y-axis represents the unit of measure, such as dollars, population size, percentage, or frequency. The horizontal or x-axis shows the data classifications.

Data and communication objectives should guide the researcher's selection of chart type. Most charts are basically some variation on one of three basic types: line, bar, and pie. Many software programs offer several possible variations on these basic types that include overlap and three-dimensional effects to produce a polished, professional appearance. The use of color is also important for vivid, attractive illustrations. Affordable color printers and overhead projection hardware for personal computers have freed public administrators from mundane "box and whisker" diagrams. If SPSS

TABLE 6.6 Illustration Objectives and Most Appropriate Chart Types

Objective	Chart Types
To describe a statistical trend in one variable or to compare trends for up to three data series over time	Line
To depict frequencies or percentages, or to compare two or three groups on an interval or ratio variable	Bar
To show changes in volume or running totals	Area
To emphasize the parts of a whole	Pie
To emphasize one part of a whole	Pie with exploded slice
To emphasize parts of a whole at two different times, or one part of a whole at two different times	Two pies or two pies with exploded slices

for Windows does not have the exact type of chart one desires, it is easy to import the data into other Windows applications, such as Microsoft Excel, to produce a wider variety of illustrations. Table 6.6 summarizes typical survey illustration objectives and the types of charts appropriate for displaying various types of information.

Line charts describe or compare trends over time. They are especially appropriate when change is dramatic. Bar charts compare specific items, such as recyclable materials or revenue sources, rather than changes over time. Pie charts emphasize the parts of a whole or compare parts over two time periods. Pie cuts, or "exploded" slices, draw attention to particularly interesting features, such as the proportion of citizens who favor spending more for economic development. Figure 6.7 shows line, bar, and pie charts that summarize selected survey findings.

Summary

Statistics are tools that researchers use to summarize survey findings and to measure relationships that help to explain behaviors, opinions, or preferences among respondents. The survey's information objectives and the number and level of measurement of the variables govern the types of statistical analyses that should be performed. Investigators must be familiar with and knowledgeable about the subjects of their surveys to detect and explain findings that are both statistically significant and substantively important.

The data analysis stage is perhaps the most exciting of the entire survey process, and not just because it represents the fruition of long hours of work. It is the stage of discovery in survey research when numbers are

Line/Area chart:

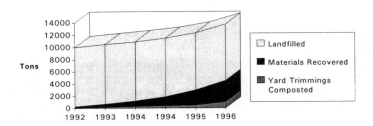

Bar chart:

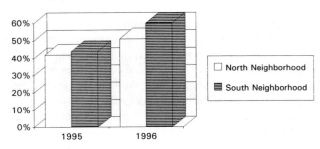

Figure 6.7. Examples of Chart Types

translated into information with the potential to inform the public policy process. How to go about summarizing this information in a final report and appropriate media releases is the subject of Chapter 7.

Notes

1. The standard deviation formula is the square root of the sum of the squared deviations of each case from the mean divided by the total number of cases:

$$s = \sqrt{\frac{\Sigma(x-\overline{X})^2}{N}} \quad .$$

Pie chart:

**Support for Metropolitan Consolidation in
River City and King County in May 1997**

River City

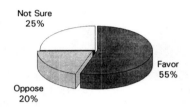

King County

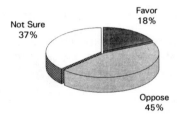

Figure 6.7. Continued

2. Multiple regression analysis is a very useful multivariate technique for variables measured at the interval level. O'Sullivan and Rassel (1995) and Johnson and Joslyn (1991) provide excellent explanations of this technique.

3. The formula for lambda is $(L - M)/L$, where L is the proportion of errors made in predicting the dependent variable not knowing the value of the independent variable, and M is the proportion of errors in predicting the dependent variable knowing the value of the independent variable.

4. Cramer's V is the square root of the result of chi-square divided by the product of the number of rows *or* columns minus 1 (whichever is smaller) times the sample size. The formula is as follows:

$$\text{Cramer's } V = \sqrt{\frac{\chi^2}{N(r-1) \text{ or } (c-1)}} \quad .$$

5. The formula for gamma is as follows: Gamma = (Number of Concordant Pairs – Discordant Pairs)/(Number of Concordant Pairs + Discordant Pairs). The formulas for tau b and tau c are adapted from Johnson and Joslyn (1991, pp. 305-306):

$$\tau b = \frac{P-Q}{\sqrt{(P+Q+T_2)(P+Q+T_1)}}$$

$$\tau c = \frac{P-Q}{\frac{1}{2}(n)^2 \left[\frac{(m-1)}{m}\right]},$$

where P is the number of concordant pairs, Q is the number of discordant pairs, T_1 is the number of ties on the row variables, T_2 is the number of ties on the column variables, m is the smaller of the number of rows and columns, and n is the number of cases in the table.

6. The chi-square formula is as follows:

$$\chi^2 = \Sigma\,(O-E)^2/E,$$

where O is the observed frequencies for each cell and E is the expected frequency in each cell. Statistical software programs report the significance level or associated probability that a chi-square value of the size computed would occur if the null hypothesis is true for the target population.

7. See O'Sullivan and Rassel (1995, pp. 353-358) for an excellent discussion of Type I and Type II errors and their practical consequences for public administrators. The following summarizes these errors:

	In Real World Null Is	
Decision	True	False
Reject null	Type I error	No error
Accept null	No error	Type II error

8. The degrees of freedom is the number of columns in the table minus 1 (i.e., C – 1) times the number of rows in the table minus 1 (i.e., R – 1).

9. The t score is derived using the following formula:

$$t = \frac{\overline{X}_1 - \overline{X}_2}{SE},$$

where the mean of the second sample is subtracted from the mean of the first sample, with the remainder divided by the overall standard error. The overall standard error is the square root of the sum of the squared standard errors of the mean estimates for each sample. The standard error of the mean estimate is the standard deviation (σ) divided by the square root of the sample size (n). Expressed mathematically:

$$\text{Standard Error } (SE) = \frac{\sigma}{\sqrt{n}}$$

$$\text{Overall Standard Error} = \sqrt{SE_1^2 + SE_2^2}\;.$$

10. See Johnson and Joslyn (1991, pp. 317-318) for examples of how the following formula for eta^2 is computed, where SS = the sum of squares:

$$\frac{\text{Total } SS - \text{Unexplained } SS}{\text{Total } SS} = \frac{\text{Explained } SS}{\text{Total } SS} .$$

11. For excellent explanations of the use of multiple regression techniques, see O'Sullivan and Rassel (1995) or Welch and Comer (1988).

12. Logit techniques are explained clearly in Demaris (1992).

13. For additional examples, see Eells (1991).

7

Preparing the Survey
Report and Media Releases

A carefully planned and well-executed survey is a fruitless exercise unless the final report clearly communicates what was done, how it was done, and what was found. The final report explains these aspects of the survey project so that consumers can judge the accuracy of the research and the utility of the findings. Media releases about the results are just as important, because most citizens learn about surveys through news coverage. Official media releases represent excellent opportunities for sponsors to describe the noteworthy findings of the project. These releases help to minimize reportorial misinterpretations and are among the first steps in a broader public discourse about what citizens think and what government officials should do in response. How well this process is managed affects later political support for action as well as citizen judgments about the value of survey participation.

The audience for the official survey report usually consists of other public administrators, elected officials, and interested citizens. The audience for press releases consists of everyone else. The needs of the two audiences are different, and the design and content of the report and media releases should reflect this fact.

The Survey Report

An effective report is well organized, clearly written, and concise. It should include a table of contents, an executive summary, an explanation of the purpose and objectives of the project, a description of the methods used to acquire the data, a description of the findings (including any charts), and a summary of the implications. Depending on the needs and expectations of the survey sponsors, an additional section may recommend actions based on the report's findings and implications.

THE EXECUTIVE SUMMARY

The executive summary is usually the last section to be written, but it is the leadoff for the report. It highlights in one or two pages the contents of the report and presents a highly condensed version of the project's purpose, methodology, and major findings. It may also include a list of recommended actions suggested by the findings. The executive summary is the section most likely to be read by busy executives who are interested mainly in an answer to the "So what?" question. Investigators should anticipate and respond to this concern by describing the chief conclusions that can be drawn from the survey results.

SURVEY OBJECTIVES

A survey planned in accordance with the guidelines recommended in Chapter 2 has a clear purpose and specific information objectives. The section of the report that describes these objectives should relate the reasons for doing the survey, what information was needed and why, and how this information was expected to inform specific types of deliberations, decisions, or actions by various actors.

METHODOLOGY

The report's methodology section should explain how the information was gathered, when it was collected, the response rate, and what the confidence level and margin of error mean in the context of the response rate to the sample. A complete copy of the questionnaire may be included in an appendix to enable readers to inspect question wording and order.

The researcher's objective in the methodology section is to present a thorough, accurate, and honest description of what he or she did and how. This section should describe the accuracy of the results in terms of the confidence level and error margin, and should explain what these concepts mean. Any weights assigned to variables should be reported, and the use of screen questions to identify respondents with particular knowledge, experience, or attributes should be noted. The quality of the research effort is distinguished by the methods employed. A well-written methodological summary will also help the next survey team replicate or refine the work that has been accomplished.

MAJOR FINDINGS

The section on the survey's major findings should summarize the results and review them in order of their importance or interest to the audience. Tables should be used to summarize the main findings, and the most interesting results should be highlighted with appropriate graphic illustrations. It is not necessary to include tables for *every* question in the survey; the profile of respondents' attributes, for instance, can be placed in an appendix.

IMPLICATIONS OF THE FINDINGS

The section that presents the implications of the survey findings is especially important, because it answers the "So what?" question. This section should discuss the deductions that are possible from the findings that relate to the objectives of the survey. Here descriptions should be offered regarding the possible changes, actions, or effects that the findings portend for the organization and how it serves its constituencies. This section should address how the survey results may affect what the organization does or should do and how it does it. The findings of the survey may be expected or unexpected; this section should explain how they confirm or challenge prevailing beliefs about popular or group opinions.

In writing this section, the investigator should be sure to distinguish findings that attain statistical significance from those that are substantively important. Findings that are statistically significant *may* be substantively important. A finding that two things are unrelated also may be substantively important. For example, if place of residence and support for metropolitan government are unrelated, this may affect a decision about whether to hold a popular referendum on the issue. Substantive importance is the golden yardstick for decision makers. No statistic can compute this quality. The analyst's knowledge, insight, and experience are the bases for recognizing important findings; statistical measures are merely the signposts in that process.

It is never sufficient just to report that several statistically significant relationships exist between independent variables such as income, race, education, or place of residence and various dependent measures such as service quality, citizen satisfaction, or support for a particular program. The implications of these findings should address the "So what?" question as it pertains to what these relationships mean for the political calculus of policy, program, and managerial decision making.

The survey findings may have implications concerning what is being done right, what is not, and how particular changes may improve, enhance, or otherwise affect the direction, quality, usefulness, or responsiveness of the policy, program, or service. In some cases, the implications may consist of little more than the need to conduct future studies to measure whether citizens' service evaluations continue to be so exceptional. Whatever is gleaned from the results, the inferences must be based on the evidence obtained, tempered by an understanding of the limits of survey research. A single survey is not a magic evaluation bullet. At best, it is a useful snapshot of opinions at a particular point in time. Periodic survey efforts provide a more complete picture over time and provide public officials with a more robust information base for decision making.

Media Releases

The decision to spend scarce resources on a survey usually means that the results should be shared with citizens. Media releases or statements are one kind of vehicle for disseminating accurate information about the survey and its findings. Even if a release is not printed or reported verbatim, it should contain the information public officials believe citizens should know.

A media release should not be viewed as an opportunity to engage in partisan "spin doctoring." Rather, it is a recognition of a responsibility to share with the public the import and implications of information obtained with their cooperation and tax dollars. Media releases should reflect the same professionalism that characterizes survey design and implementation.

The executive summary of the final report provides a good starting point for the drafting of a release. To enable a nontechnical audience to assess the accuracy of the findings, the release should describe the following methodological points:

- Who was surveyed, when they were contacted, the method of contact, and the size of the sample
- The sample's error range and confidence level, illustrated by an example of what these concepts mean
- The response rate

The release also should identify the sponsors of the survey and who conducted it (e.g., government employees or a private consultant under contract). The full text of the questions reviewed in the release should be included, presented in the order they appear in the instrument, to allow readers to judge whether question wording or order may bias the results. In an era when many of the surveys people encounter are unscientific, this information will help to distinguish the survey from the nonscientific, "person-on-the-street" polls commonly reported in the media.

When reporting the opinion distribution for a question, the release should include the "base" upon which the percentages are computed. The numbers of missing cases or nonresponses to questions should also be reported. "Truth in statistics" requires the public administrator to report the number of people who chose a "don't know or not sure" response. For example, it is one thing to say that 55% of citizens favor consolidation and 45% oppose it, but it is quite another to say that 39% favor it, 31% oppose it, and 30% don't know or are not sure. The base of the first distribution consists of the 700 respondents who expressed an opinion in a survey of 1,000 citizens. The second distribution includes the 300 citizens in the same survey who answered the question with a "no opinion" response. Obviously, the conclusions reached by the reader will depend on the base used to calculate the distribution. Clearly, the base matters.

Some or all of the information included in media releases may be edited by print and broadcast journalists, but public administrators cannot expect improvements in popular reports of surveys unless they treat these elements as standard items in their releases. Figure 7.1 presents a hypothetical example

What Do King County Citizens Think About Metropolitan Consolidation?

During May 22-28, planning office staff, under the supervision of Director Fred Olmstead, conducted telephone interviews with a randomly selected sample of 625 adults 18 and older in King County households to inquire whether they favor or oppose consolidation of River City and King County governments.

Citizens were asked: "If a vote were taken this week, would you favor or oppose consolidation of the River City and King County governments into one metropolitan government?" The percent distribution for all responses follows:

All Respondents' Opinions on Consolidation	*Percent*
Favor	40
Oppose	30
Don't Know/ Not Sure	30
Total	100% (N= 625)

The planning staff compared the opinions of the 375 respondents who live in River City with the 250 respondents who live outside the corporate limits in King County. The findings showed the following:

Opinion on Consolidation	*River City*		*King County*	
	N	%	N	%
Favor	206	55	44	18
Oppose	75	20	113	45
Don't Know or Not Sure	94	25	93	37
Total	375	100%	250	100%

The planning staff point out in their report to the Joint Commission for Consolidation (the survey sponsors) that if a vote on consolidation had occurred during the week of the survey, it would have been approved in the city and defeated in the county.

The households selected were chosen by random digit dialing to ensure that all households had an equal chance of being interviewed. The number of households contacted was proportional to the number of residential phone lines in each region of the county. At least four callback attempts were made to each working telephone number at different times and days before it was replaced with another randomly generated number in the exchange.

The random sample of 625 households means that researchers are 95% certain that between 36% and 44% of all citizens favor consolidation. This represents a margin of error of plus or minus 4 percentage points. The error margins for the opinion estimates of what city or county residents think about consolidation are somewhat higher (5.2% and 6.3%, respectively).

Figure 7.1. Hypothetical Press Release

of a press release for a survey about citizens' opinions on metropolitan consolidation.

Summary

Almost two decades ago, Dillman (1978) worried that "survey mania" would result in "thousands of ill-advised and poorly constructed surveys that produce results of no use to anyone" (p. 296). Regrettably, this observation has proved to be prophetic. The number of poorly designed surveys currently being conducted by groups and individuals who really should know better is appalling. More worrisome still is the increasingly common misuse of surveys by those who lack any scientific or ethical scruples. The former case limits the utility and value of survey results and wastes resources. The latter inflicts incalculable damage on the implicit trust that underlies the exchange relationship between citizens and responsible survey researchers and jeopardizes the credibility of surveys as a method of accurate information acquisition.

Responsible researchers abide by the ethical practices prescribed by the American Association for Public Opinion Research. A good-faith effort to apply these practices and the guidelines described in each of the stages of the survey research process will help the researcher to obtain information that is useful, accurate, and appropriate to the purposes of the project at hand. Only hindsight is perfect, however. The final report of the survey should describe any problems, errors, or insights that may help others to assess the survey's quality and to learn from the researcher's experiences.

The future utility of survey research depends on the professionalism that each practitioner brings to the tasks of survey design, implementation, and reporting of results. The final report and media releases should reflect this professional concern for quality, reliability, and validity. These collective efforts shape the legacy that will be left to future generations of survey researchers and affect the potential of surveys to be a reliable basis for translating popular preferences into government actions.

APPENDIX A
Random Numbers Table

74397	99019	02529	09376	70715	38311	31165	88676	27659	04436
93433	98520	17767	14905	68607	22109	40558	60970	73998	50500
09117	10097	32533	76520	13586	34673	54876	80959	74945	39292
10402	37542	04805	64894	74296	24805	24037	20636	91665	00822
34764	09422	68953	19645	09303	23209	02560	15953	33606	35080
07439	31060	10805	45571	82406	35303	42614	86799	09732	23403
85247	85269	77602	02051	65692	68665	74818	73053	88579	18623
16877	12807	99970	80156	36174	60342	53663	98752	33768	12711
28709	63573	32135	05325	47048	90553	57548	28468	25624	83491
20344	73796	45753	03529	62778	35808	14282	60935	88435	35273
24201	11805	05431	39808	27732	50725	68248	29405	67851	52775
60008	45974	75158	94918	40144	31460	22219	18804	97923	57562
40610	83452	99634	06288	98083	13746	70078	18175	77817	68711
76493	88685	40200	86507	58401	36766	67951	90364	11062	29609
61368	99594	67348	87517	64969	91826	08928	93785	34113	23478
57186	65481	17674	17468	50950	58007	76974	73039	44561	40218
78253	80124	35635	17727	08015	45318	22374	21115	53763	14385
64237	74350	99817	77402	77211	43236	00210	45022	02655	96286
13990	69916	26803	66252	29148	36936	87203	76621	56418	94400
78822	09893	20505	14225	00802	46427	56788	96297	89541	54382
89923	91459	14523	68479	27686	46162	83554	94750	20048	37089
33340	80336	94598	26940	36858	70297	34135	53140	82341	42050
40881	44114	81949	85157	43954	32979	26575	57670	06413	22222
89439	12552	73742	11100	02040	12860	74697	96644	25815	28707
77082	63606	49329	16505	34484	40219	52563	43651	31790	07204
59093	61286	90646	26357	47774	51924	31229	65394	60527	42582
10118	15474	45266	95270	79953	59367	83848	82396	59466	33211
42592	94557	28573	67897	84387	54622	44431	91190	45973	92927
12059	42481	16213	97344	08721	16868	48767	03071	46670	25701
29663	23523	78317	73209	89837	68935	91416	26252	82562	03522
79335	10918	52494	75246	33824	45862	51025	61962	12472	65337
82391	00549	97654	64051	28159	35464	63896	54692	29529	23287
50024	35963	15307	26898	09354	33351	35462	77974	39333	90103
24892	59808	08391	45427	26842	83609	49700	13021	20106	78565
85647	85064	85236	01039	93286	77281	44077	93910	14294	70617

APPENDIX B
Call Sheet

Interviewer's Name:_____

Project: _____   Sample Area: _____

Disposition Codes:
- BG - Business/Government Office
- BZ - Busy
- CB - Callback
- CM - Completed
- DL - Deaf/Language Barrier
- DS - Disconnected
- NA - No Answer
- NR - Nonresident
- RF - Refusal
- TM - Terminated

Phone Number	1st Attempt			2nd Attempt			3rd Attempt			4th Attempt		
	Date	Time	Code	Date	Time	Code	Date	Time	Code	Date	Time	Code
_____												
_____												
_____												
_____												
_____												
_____												
_____												
_____												

References

American Association for Public Opinion Research. (1986). *Code of professional ethics and practices*. Ann Arbor: Author.

Asher, H. (1988). *Polling and the public: What every citizen should know*. Washington, DC: Congressional Quarterly.

Babbie, E. R. (1995). *The practice of social research*. Belmont, CA: Wadsworth.

Belson, W. A. (1986). *Validity in survey research*. Aldershot, England: Gower.

Biemer, P. P., Groves, R. M., Lyberg, L. E., Mathiowetz, N. A., & Sudman, S. S. (Eds.). (1991). *Measurement errors in surveys*. New York: John Wiley.

Blalock, H. M. (1979). *Social statistics* (2nd ed.). New York: McGraw-Hill.

Blankenship, A. B. (1940). The influence of the question form upon the response in a public opinion poll. *Psychological Record, 3,* 345-422.

Bradburn, N. M., & Sudman, S. S. (1991). The current status of questionnaire design. In P. P. Biemer, R. M. Groves, L. E. Lyberg, N. A. Mathiowetz, & S. S. Sudman (Eds.), *Measurement errors in surveys* (pp. 29-40). New York: John Wiley.

Converse, J. M., & Presser, S. (1986). *Survey questions: Handcrafting the standardized questionnaire*. Beverly Hills, CA: Sage.

Demaris, A. (1992). *Logit modeling: Practical applications*. Newbury Park, CA: Sage.

Dexter, L. A. (1970). *Elite and specialized interviewing*. Evanston, IL: Northwestern University Press.

Dillman, D. A. (1978). *Mail and telephone surveys: The total design method*. New York: John Wiley.

181

Eells, E. (1991). *Probabilistic causality.* Cambridge: Cambridge University Press.

Fowler, F. J. (1993). *Survey research methods.* Newbury Park, CA: Sage.

Frey, J. H. (1989). *Survey research by telephone.* Newbury Park, CA: Sage.

Groves, R. M., Biemer, P. P., Lyberg, L. E., Massey, J. T., Nicholls, W. L., & Waksberg, J. (1988). *Telephone survey methodology.* New York: John Wiley.

Hessler, R. M. (1992). *Social research methods.* St. Paul, MN: West.

Johnson, J. B., & Joslyn, R. A. (1991). *Political science research methods.* Washington, DC: Congressional Quarterly.

Kiesler, S., & Sproull, L. S. (1986). Response effects in the electronic survey. *Public Opinion Quarterly, 50,* 402-413.

Kimmel, A. J. (1988). *Ethics and values in applied social research.* Newbury Park, CA: Sage.

Lavrakas, P. J. (1987). *Telephone survey methods.* Newbury Park, CA: Sage.

Meier, J. M., & Brudney, J. L. (1993). *Applied statistics for public administration.* Belmont, CA: Wadsworth.

Miller, T., & Miller, M. (1991). *Citizen surveys: How to do them, how to use them, what they mean.* Washington, DC: ICMA.

Morgan, D. L. (1993). *Successful focus groups.* Newbury Park, CA: Sage.

Morin, R. (1995, February 26). Lucky stars. *Washington Post,* p. C5.

Nachmias, C. F., & Nachmias, D. (1992). *Research methods in the social sciences.* New York: St. Martin's.

Norpoth, H., & Lodge, M. (1985). The difference between attitudes and nonattitudes in the mass public: Just measurement? *American Journal of Political Science, 29,* 291-307.

Oppenheim, A. N. (1992). *Questionnaire design, interviewing and attitude measurement.* London: Pinter.

O'Sullivan, E., & Rassel, G. R. (1995). *Research methods for public administrators.* New York: Longman.

Payne, S. L. (1951). *The art of asking questions.* Princeton, NJ: Princeton University Press.

Poister, T. H. (1978). *Public program analysis: Applied research methods.* Baltimore: University Park Press.

Rubenstein, S. M. (1995). *Surveying public opinion.* Belmont, CA: Wadsworth.

Schmid, C. F. (1983). *Statistical graphics: Design principles and practices.* New York: John Wiley.

Schuman, H., & Presser, S. (1981). *Questions and answers in attitude surveys: Experiments on question form, wording, and context.* New York: Academic Press.

Schwarz, N., & Hippler, H. (1991). Response alternatives: The impact of their choice and presentation order. In P. P. Biemer, R. M. Groves, L. E. Lyberg, N. A. Mathiowetz, & S. S. Sudman (Eds.), *Measurement errors in surveys* (pp. 41-56). New York: John Wiley.

Singleton, R. A., Jr., Straits, B. A., & Straits, M. (1993). *Approaches to social research.* New York: Oxford University Press.

Sudman, S. S., & Bradburn, N. M. (1974). *Response effects in surveys.* Chicago: Aldine.

Sudman, S. S., & Bradburn, N. M. (1982). *Asking questions: A practical guide to questionnaire design.* San Francisco: Jossey-Bass.

Weisberg, H. F., Krosnick, J. A., & Bowen, B. D. (1989). *An introduction to survey research and data analysis.* Glenview, IL: Scott, Foresman.

Welch, S., & Comer, J. (1988). *Quantitative methods for public administration.* Chicago: Dorsey.

Yamane, T. (1967). *Elementary sampling theory.* Englewood Cliffs, NJ: Prentice Hall.

Index

Accuracy:
  in data entry, 136
  in reporting results, 45-46, 174
  of samples, 38, 43, 47-49
  of survey research methods, 33
Acquiescence response set bias, 88-89
Administrative costs, 36
Alpha levels, 156
American Association for Public Opinion
  Research, 9, 178
American Review of Public Administration,
  78
Analysis:
  bivariate data, 147-162
  multivariate data, 162-165
  univariate data, 141-147
Analysis of variance, 159-160
Anonymity, 115-116
Appearance:
  of charts, 166

  of questionnaire, 93, 109
Asher, H., 18
Association:
  measures of, 152-159
Asymmetric measures, 154
Attitude questions, 20
Attitudes, 16-20
Attribute questions, 26, 78, 91
Attributes:
  as dependent variables, 25
  as independent variables, 25
  importance of, 24-25, 27
  mutually exclusive, 84
  of question types, 88
  population, 43
  respondents, 39, 43, 174
  responses, 73

Babbie, E. R., 27, 28, 47, 59, 63, 138

Background questions, 26
Bar charts, 166-168
Behavior questions, 23
Behaviors, 21-24
Belief questions, 22
Beliefs, 21
Belson, W. A., 91
Bias:
    acquiescence response set, 88-89
    instrumentation, 88
    interviewing, 61, 88
    question wording, 87-91
    sampling, 54-57
    social desirability, 23, 89-91
    straight-line response set, 89
Biased questions:
    examples of, 97-100
Biemer, P., 91
Birthday method, 72-73
Bivariate relationships, 147-159, 164-165
Blalock, H. M., 60, 138
Blankenship, N. M., 91
Bowen, B. D., 66, 90, 141
Bradburn, N. M., 81, 91, 120
Brudney, J. L., 138
Budget:
    for surveys, 34-36

Call-back sheets, Appendix B, 180
Call-in polls, 56
CAPI, 136
CATI, 134-136
Causality, 162, 164-165
CBS-*New York Times* Poll, 78
CD-ROM, 69
Census, 25, 39, 57, 70, 78
Central tendency, 141-1142, 144-145
Chart types:
    illustrations, 67
Chi-square, 169-170
Citizen participation, 7
Citizen surveys:
    inappropriate uses of, 7-9

purpose of, 2-7
uses, 3-7
Clarity:
    of questionnaire items, 77, 97-101
Cleaning data, 136-137
Closed-ended questions:
    examples, 83-86
    with ordered choices, 85
    with unordered choices, 85
Cluster samples, 61-65
Codebook, 132
Code of ethics, 9, 178
Coding:
    procedures for, 128
    open-ended items, 131-132
    scheme, 130-131
Cohort study, 29-30
Collapsing interval data, 142
Comer, J., 171
Compensation:
    of callers, 124
Composition standards, 96-103
Computer-assisted personal interviews
    (CAPI), 136
Computer-assisted telephone interviewing
    (CATI), 134-136
Computer:
    data files, 12, 128-130, 132-134
    personal, 127, 129, 135, 166
Concepts:
    operationalization of, 28, 78, 96-101,
        105-109, 140
Confidence interval, 47-49
Confidence level, 47-49
Confidentiality, 9, 24, 34, 38, 112-116
Contingency tables, 148- 152
Control variables, 162-165
Converse, J. M., 79, 92, 120, 122
Correlation:
    Pearson's product-moment, 155, 161-162
Cost:
    comparisons, 34-36
    of mail surveys, 35-36
    of personal interviews, 36

of telephone surveys, 36
Cover letter, 109, 113-114
Cramer's V, 149, 153-154, 157-158, 165,
    169
Criterion:
    probability, 156, 160
Cross-sectional study, 15, 29
Cross-tabulations, 148-152

Data:
    access to, 115-116
    analysis, 12
    cleaning, 136-137
    entry, 132-136
    file, 134
    processing, 128-130
    sources, 9
Degrees of freedom, 158, 160, 170
Demaris, A., 171
Demographics, 25, 39
Dependent variables, 25, 60, 105-109, 147-
    148, 175
Descriptive statistics, 139, 144
Design:
    research, 29-30
    sampling, 52-54
Dexter, L. A., 40
Dichotomous variables, 155
Difference of means, 159-161
Dillman, D. A., 1117, 33, 90, 92, 110, 119,
    120, 125, 178
Direction of association, 148, 150, 152,
    154, 157-158
Dispersion:
    measures of, 144-145
Disproportionate sampling and weighting,
    50, 65-67
Disproportionate stratified sampling, 61
Distributions:
    frequency, 142-143
    percent, 142-143
Double-barreled questions, 88, 97-99
Double negatives, 100

Ecological fallacy, 30-31
Eells, E., 171
Elaboration modeling, 164-165
Elements:
    sampling, 63
Elites:
    strategies for interviewing,
        39-41
Environmental activism, 107-108
Errors:
    human, 124, 130
    measurement, 74
    non-sampling, 74
    sampling, 44-45
    standard, 45
Eta-squared, 160
Ethics:
    and confidentiality, 9
    in reporting, 178
Evaluation:
    citizen, 4-8
    of services, 8
    research, 4-7
Excel®, 129, 167
Exchange:
    relationship, 92, 178
Executive summary, 173
Experiments:
    survey, 18, 27
Explained variance, 160
Explanation, 165
Explanatory questions, 16
Exploratory questions, 16, 82, 88
Extreme scores, 144

Face-to-face interviewing, 32-34
Face validity, 106
Facts, 24-26
Fallacy:
    ecological, 30-31
False assumptions, 98
Field:
    researchers in, 36-37

Files:
    data, 129-130
    merging, 130
Findings:
    implications of, 174-175
Focus groups, 28-29
Forced-choice questions, 83
Format:
    for call-back sheets, 74
    for questionnaires, 109-110
Fowler, F. J., 121
F-ratio, 160
Frequency distribution, 142
Frey, J. H., 34, 67, 68, 72, 73, 119, 120
Frugging, 9
F-test, 149
Funnel sequence, 104

Gallup poll, 56, 78
Gamma, 153-155, 170
Gender differences, 39, 67, 72
Goals:
    community, 16
    survey, 14-17
Goodness of fit, 161
Groups:
    as units of analysis, 16, 30
Groves, R. M., 67, 91

Hippler, H., 85
Hit rate, 70
Households:
    as unit of analysis, 71-72
Hypothesis:
    null, 156
    testing, 156

Implementation time, 37
Independent variables, 25, 141, 147-148,
    175
Indexes, 105-109

Indicators, 105-106
Inducements, 92-95, 109-110
Inferences, 42, 47
Inferential statistics, 139-140, 148, 155-156
Information:
    needs, 26-30
    types, 19-26
Informed consent, 9, 117
Instrumentation bias, 88
Interpretation:
    in elaboration modeling, 165
Interquartile range, 144-145
Interval level of measurement, 140-141
Intervening variable, 165
Interviewer:
    characteristics of, 37, 116-117
    supervision of, 124-125
    training of, 123-125
Interview guide, 40-41
Interviews:
    elite or specialized, 39-41
    face-to-face, 32-38
    telephone, 32-38
Introductory spiel, 117-118
Inverted funnel sequence, 104
Item analysis, 108

Johnson, J. B., 40, 41, 45, 153, 160, 169,
    170, 171
Joslyn, R. A., 40, 41, 45, 153, 160, 169,
    170, 171
Journalists, 176

Kendall's tau-b, 154-155, 170
Kendall's tau-c, 154-155, 170
Key-word summary, 116, 119
Kiesler, S., 136
Kimmel, A. J., 115
Knowledge:
    respondent, 4, 17-19
Krosnick, J. A., 66, 90, 141

Lambda, 149, 153-154
Lavrakas, P. J., 70, 72
Leading questions, 101-102
Level of confidence, 47-49
Level of significance, 156
Levels of measurement, 140-141
Likert scale, 94, 109, 131, 136
Literature review, 15, 78-79
Loaded questions, 88, 101-102
Lodge, M., 18
Logic:
    sampling, 43-46
    survey, 2-7
Logit, 163
Longitudinal studies, 29-30

Mail surveys:
    cover letter for, 109-110, 113, 114
    design of, 109-112
    implementation of, 112-115
    length, 17, 32, 34-35, 110
    processing, 112-115
    response rate, 38
Matrix:
    question format, 119
Mean, 144
Measurement:
    levels of, 140-141
    principles, 84
    reliability of, 3, 11, 79, 83, 102
Measures:
    of association, 149
    of dispersion, 144
Median, 144
Media releases, 175-178
Meier, J. M., 138
Memory burden, 102, 116, 122-123
Miller, M., 31, 33
Miller, T., 31, 33
Misuse of surveys, 7-9
Mock interviews, 125
Mode, 144
Morgan, D. L., 28

Morin, R., 18
Motivation:
    of respondents, 17-19, 92-95
Multiple regression, 163
Multistage cluster sampling, 62-66
Multivariate analysis, 162-165
Mutually exclusive categories, 84

Nachmias, C. F., 51, 74
Nachmias, D., 51, 74
National Opinion Research Center
    (NORC), 78
Nominal:
    measures, 140, 153-154
    variables, 140
Nonattitudes:
    problems with, 17-19
Nonprobability sampling, 54-57
Nonresponses:
    strategies for dealing with, 38-39
Nonsampling error, 74
Nonzero probability, 46
Normal curve, 46-47, 49
Norpoth, C. F., 18
Null hypothesis, 156

Objectivity:
    politics of survey research and, 7-9
Observations:
    units of, 30
Open-ended questions, 81-82, 88
Operational definitions, 106
Opinions:
    questions on, 19-20
Oppenheim, A. N., 92
Ordered choices, 85-86, 88
Ordering of questions, 80-81, 103-105, 118-
    120
Ordinal variables, 140
Organizing staff, 11, 123-1125
O'Sullivan, E., 49, 51, 138, 169, 170, 171

Panel study, 30
Partially closed-ended questions, 84-85, 98
Payne, S. L., 78, 91, 101, 120
Pearson *r* value, 161-162
Peer review, 14-16, 80, 82, 95
Penetration rate, 68
Percentages:
    valid, 146-147
Percent distribution, 142-143
Perceptions:
    citizen, 5-6
    measuring, 21-22
Periodicity, 59, 66
Person on the street interview, 56
Personnel:
    requirements, 36-37
Pie charts, 167, 169
Planning:
    advantages of, 9-10, 14
    process, 9-10, 14-17
Poister, T. H., 154
Population:
    parameter, 43-44
    proportions, 48
    sampling frame, 32
    size, 49
    small, 49-50
    target, 30
PRE (proportional reduction of error), 153
Precision, 3, 48-49
Prediction, 153-154
Presser, S., 18
Press release, 177
Pretesting, 11-12, 120-123
Priming effects, 104
Probability:
    sampling, 43-46
    theory, 46
Probability proportionate to size (PPS), 63-65
Probe questions, 40
Processing sampling pools, 73-74
Public Administration Review, 78
Public opinion:

    measuring, 19-20, 105-109
Public Opinion Quarterly, 78
Purpose of surveys, 1, 3-7, 14-17

Quality control, 54, 73-74, 120-121, 136-137, 174
Questionnaire:
    booklet, 110-112
    design of, 109-112
    identification numbers for, 112
    implementation of, 112-115
    instructions for, 109
    self-administered, 35
    structure of, 80-81, 103-105, 110-112
    timing of mailings, 115
    visual appeal of, 110-112
Questions:
    biased, 87-91
    categories, 83-85
    clarity, 97-101
    closed-ended, 83-85
    complexity, 96
    demanding, 24, 82
    double-barreled, 97, 99
    double negatives, 100
    filter, 15, 18-19
    first, 103-104, 118-119
    instructions for, 77-78, 84
    matrix, 119
    open-ended, 81-82
    order, 80-81, 103-105
    pretesting, 120-123
    screen, 18-20, 32, 63, 71-73, 99-100
    structure, 81-85
    symmetry, 102
    time referents, 102
    types, 81-85
    vertical flow, 77, 109, 115, 123
    wording effects, 101-102
    writing, 78-81, 91-92
Quota sampling, 56-57

Random digit dialing (RDD), 68-69
Random numbers table, Appendix A, 179
  use of, 58-59
Random sampling, 57-69
Random selection, 57-65
Range, 144-145
Rank ordering information objectives, 15-17
Rassel, G. R., 49, 51, 138, 169, 170, 171
Ratio measures, 140-141
Refusal rates, 38, 70
Relationships:
  among variables, 147-151
  causal, 162-165
  spurious, 165
  strength of, 148-149
Reliability, 3, 78, 83, 102
Replication:
  in elaboration modeling, 164-165
  of surveys, 29, 174
Reports:
  of survey results, 166, 173-175
Representative sample, 43
Research:
  questions, 3-7, 29-30
Respondents:
  selection of, 30-32, 43-46
Response categories:
  number of, 96, 102
Response rate:
  calculation of, 74-75
Response sets:
  composing, 96-103
Reverse directory, 69
Rewards, 93-94
Rubenstein, S. M., 9, 92, 116

Sample size, 46-52
Sampling:
  accuracy, 43-46
  bias, 54-57
  cluster, 61-65

costs, 45, 47-49
definition of, 10-11, 42-43
designs, 52-54
directories, 57-59
error, 44
fraction, 46
frame, 32
goals, 43, 49
lists, 52-53
methods, 57-65
multistage cluster, 61-66
pool, 57
simple random, 57-58
stratified random, 59-61
systematic selection, 58-59
unit, 42
Sampling pool:
  estimating size, 70-71
  processing of, 73-74
Sawtooth Software, 135
Scales:
  Likert, 94, 109, 131, 136
Schimd, C. F., 166
Schuman, H., 18
Schwarz, N., 85
Scientific method, 2
Scientific sampling, 10, 43-46
Screening respondents, 71-73
Screen questions, 18-20, 32, 63, 71-73, 99-100
Simple random sampling, 57-58
Simpson's paradox, 163
Single-stage cluster sampling, 62
Singleton, R. A., 52, 53
Size:
  of sample, 46-52
Skip patterns, 123
Small populations, 49-50
Social desirability bias, 89-90
Social Science Quarterly, 78
Specialized interviews, 40
Specification, 165
Spreadsheet format, 129
Sproull, L. S., 136

SPSS for Windows®:
  correlation, 162
  creating a data file in, 129-130
  crosstabs, 149-151, 156-159
  frequencies, 145-147
  missing values, 130
Standard deviation, 144-145
Standard error, 45
Standards:
  composition, 96-103
Statements, 89
Statistic, 44
Statistical significance, 155-156
Statistics:
  interpretation of, 149, 152-162
  primer for, 138-141
  selection of, 148-149
Straits, B. A., 52
Straits, M., 52
Stratified samples, 59-61
Subgroups:
  analysis of, 50
Subsamples, 59-60, 66-67
Substantive significance, 138-139
Sudman, S. S., 81, 91, 120
Sugging, 9
Survey research:
  misuses, 7-9
  process, 9-12
  purposes of, 3-7, 14-17
Surveys:
  advantages of, 2
  comparison of types, 32-38
  limitations of, 17-19
  objectives, 14-17
Surveys as participation mechanisms, 7
Symmetric measures, 154
Symmetry, 102-103
Systematic sampling, 58-59

Tables:
  proper construction of, 148-149, 152
Target population, 30-32

Task difficulty, 122-123
Tau-b, 154-155
Tau-c, 154-155
Telephone answering machines, 74
Tests of statistical significance, 149, 155-156
Time references, 102
Training interviewers, 123-125
Transition statements, 93, 95, 109, 116, 120, 123
Trend study, 29
Trust, 117
t statistic 160
t-test, 160
Type I error, 156
Type II error, 156

U.S. Census, 25, 39, 57, 70, 78
Unbiased sample, 11
Unit of analysis, 30
Univariate analysis, 141-147
Unlisted numbers, 53, 67
Unordered response choices, 85
Unstated criteria, 100-101

Validity, 3, 11, 78
Variables:
  attribute, 24-26
  control, 162-165
  definition of, 106
  dependent, 25, 60, 105-109, 147-148, 175
  dichotomous, 155
  independent, 25, 141, 147-148, 175
  interval level, 140-141
  measurement of, 139-141
  nominal, 140
  ordinal, 140
  relationship among, 148-165
Variable names:
  for SPSS, 130
Variance, 144-145

Vertical flow, 77, 109, 115, 123
Voluntary cooperation, 92-93
Volunteers:
    as survey participants, 55-56
    for conducting interviews, 36, 124
Voting, 90, 101

Weighting cases, 65-67
Weisberg, H. F., 66, 90, 141
Welch, S., 171

Yamane, T. 52, 53

About the Author

David H. Folz is Associate Professor and M.P.A. Coordinator in the Department of Political Science at the University of Tennessee, Knoxville, where he also received his Ph.D. in political science. He teaches graduate seminars in research methods and public management and undergraduate classes in state politics, urban politics, and public administration. He frequently designs surveys in connection with his research projects, and these have appeared in several professional journals, including *Public Administration Review, American Review of Public Administration, Social Science Quarterly, State and Local Government Review, Public Productivity Review,* and *Public Administration Quarterly.* He also consults on survey projects administered by the UTK Social Science Research Institute and the UTK Energy, Environment, and Resources Center.

ADV 3527